THE
MYSTERY OF LOVE
FOR THE
SINGLE

"But I would have you to be without solicitude. He that is without a wife, is solicitous for the things that belong to the Lord, how he may please God. But he that is with a wife, is solicitous for the things of the world, how he may please his wife: and he is divided."

—1 Corinthians 7:32-33

THE
MYSTERY OF LOVE
FOR THE
SINGLE

A GUIDE FOR THOSE WHO FOLLOW THE
SINGLE VOCATION IN THE WORLD

By

Fr. Dominic J. Unger,
O.F.M. Cap., S.T.L., S.S.L.

*"For I have espoused you to one
husband that I may present you as
a chaste virgin to Christ."*
—2 Corinthians 11:2

TAN BOOKS AND PUBLISHERS, INC.
Rockford, Illinois 61105

Nihil Obstat: Very Rev. Firmin Schmidt, O.F.M. Cap.
                   Censor Librorum

Imprimi Potest: Very Rev. Claude Vogel, O.F.M. Cap.
                   Minister Provincial, Province of St. Augustine

Imprimatur   ✠ Samuel Cardinal Stritch
                   Archbishop of Chicago
                   April 2, 1958

TAN BOOKS AND PUBLISHERS, INC.
P.O. Box 424
Rockford, Illinois 61105
2005

"I HAVE BEEN espoused to Him whom the Angels serve, at whose beauty the sun and moon are in admiration. My Lord Jesus Christ has given me His ring as a pledge, and has adorned me with a wreath as His spouse."

—Words of St. Agnes
From the Mass for the
Consecration of Virgins
(See pp. 55, 79)

CONTENTS

5

THE
MYSTERY OF LOVE
FOR THE
SINGLE

"And I John saw the holy city, the new Jerusalem, coming down out of heaven from God, prepared as a bride adorned for her husband." —Apocalypse 21:2

PREFACE

EVEN IN OUR SMALLER PARISHES THERE ARE MEN AND WOMEN who never intend to get married. In our larger parishes there are many such people. And the number of these is growing. Some must remain unmarried by force of circumstances. But today many are freely choosing this vocation because they are interested in a career that is less compatible with married life.

Many, indeed, of these single men and women grasp the dignity of their vocation and live it courageously and cheerfully. They do not waste their years in regret for not having been able to marry or for having passed by the vocation of marriage. Nor do they devote themselves merely to a career. They dedicate themselves primarily to a more intimate and undivided love of Christ and His Mystical Body. Some people live their single lives in the world with inner joy and peace, it is true; but they seem to have a sense of inferiority.

The present book is an attempt to help such generous souls to appreciate the excellence of their vocation as a true calling of Christ, and to realize the greatest personal merit and social blessings from that vocation. The book has in mind not only women but men as well. So throughout the work both men and women are referred to, even though only the masculine nouns and pronouns are used, or even though only the feminine pronoun is used with

9

"virgin" or "bride," unless the very nature of the statement limits the matter to either sex.

There are single people who live a life of perfect chastity and of devotion to fellow men, but who leave the door of their heart ajar, if ever so slightly, so that if some one who would seem to be the fulfillment of a dream should come along, he or she may enter. For those this book is not written, unless it be as an invitation to consider the more excellent vocation of closing the door completely and dedicating themselves to Christ irrevocably in perfect chastity.

Neither does this work aim at describing the destiny of the single man and woman in the modern world, namely, in regard to their contributions to society by careers. Much less does it propose doing this for the single woman alone. Not that such a book, if still unwritten, would not be most desirable and useful. It would, indeed. But that is not my present field of interest. I am interested in the single vocation of people in the world who have determined to dedicate their lifetime to Christ in perfect chastity. For such a person his or her career and contribution to society is great, but his or her perfect dedication to Christ and contribution of glory to Christ is greater, just as charity toward God is greater than charity toward fellow men. And these people deserve to have the subject treated directly from their viewpoint, instead of being touched upon only indirectly or by way of appendix in a general treatise on virginity, which is meant directly or chiefly for the clergy and religious.

We shall, however, devote some attention to the question of the apostolic life and career of the Christ-dedicated bachelor and virgin, first, to meet the objection that the single life of a bachelor or virgin is selfish and anti-social; secondly, to explain how such single people can really make an immense contribution to society as well as to the Church. A more specific treatment of the contribution of men and especially of women to society in the modern world is beyond the scope of this book.

At first reading certain sections of this book might seem to advocate segregating single people from the society in which they live. Nothing could be further from the truth. True, the vocation of single persons in perfect chastity in the world is a distinct vocation. As such it distinguishes single persons from the married, and this has some effects also on their social life. It would be a mistake, however, to think that such single people are to be completely segregated from society, though living in it, perhaps as a kind of secret society of their own with an anti-social attitude. As we shall explain at length, they are to live in the world just as their married brothers and sisters, and through a career they are to make their contribution to society and to the Church, though by their inner spiritual calling and striving they are distinct from the rest.

This book is meant primarily for those single people in the world who never intend to marry; but it can be adapted by widows and widowers, and penitents too. It can be useful even to those whose marriage partner has deserted permanently and irreparably, thus leaving them bound by a valid bond but forced to live a single life in regard to chastity.

To prevent the book from taking on too formidable an appearance, I have tried to keep the footnotes to a minimum. I should like here to make a general acknowledgment of special indebtedness to three studies: Dietrich von Hildenbrand, *In Defense of Purity: An Analysis of the Catholic Ideals of Purity and Virginity* (New York, Sheed and Ward, 1934, 196 pp.), Francisco de B. Vizmanos, S.J., *Las Vírgenes Cristianas de la Iglesia Primitiva: Estudio histórico-ideológico seguido de una Antología de tratados patrísticos sobre la virginidad* (Madrid, Biblioteca de Autores Cristianos, 1949, xxiv-1306 pp.), Bishop Josephus Meile, *Die Jungfräulichen Seelen in der Welt* (Dritten-ordenszentrale, Schwyz, 1950, 383 pp.).

It is hoped that the book may be at least a weak instrument in the hands of the Divine Bridegroom to help people to choose this vocation and to live it wisely, joyfully, and fruitfully, in preparation for the heavenly life of more intimate love and deeper joy with Jesus Christ, through endless ages.

THE AUTHOR

May 1, 1957
Feast of St. Joseph
the Worker

CHAPTER ONE

The Mystery of God's Love for Man

GOD IS LOVE. THAT IS THE MOST PROFOUND AND PREGNANT description of God that has ever been given. It was inspired by God Himself in the First Letter of St. John, the Beloved Disciple. "God is love," he repeated several times (1 John 4,8.16).

God is love in Himself. God loves Himself with an infinite love. That is a very profound mystery. In the Most Blessed Trinity there is the Father, who in an ineffable manner eternally begets the Son, and loves this Son of His with an infinite love. The Son on His part loves the Father with an infinite love. This mutual, infinite love of the Father and the Son is eternal: it had no beginning; it will have no end. This mutual, infinite, eternal love of the Father and the Son *is* the Third Person of the Blessed Trinity, the Holy Spirit. He is the Spirit of love, because He proceeds from both the Father and the Son by way of love.

That is, in short, the mystery of love in God Himself. We can grasp it but faintly. It will always be a mystery for us, as much as the Trinity Itself, with which it is most intimately and necessarily connected. But the little that we can understand about it is sufficient for us to realize that God is love, and that the mystery of love is at the very heart of the divine life of the Trinity.

God is love not only in Himself but also toward others. God who is infinitely perfect and happy, wanting in nothing whatever, chose, with absolute freedom and out of the superabundance of His love, to communicate some of His goodness to others. But there were no others. God, therefore, chose to create out of nothing beings to whom He might communicate His immense goodness. Knowing that variety is delightful, He created a variety of beings: material beings (the inanimate creatures and the animals), and spiritual beings (the angels), and material-spiritual beings (men).

Such, in general, is God's creation, which received an abundant outpouring of His love. We must stress that God was lavish with His love toward His creatures not because He was in want of and seeking greater love and happiness. No. He was eternally, infinitely happy and perfect. He needed no creature love. He created beings simply because of His overflowing love that freely willed to share love with others. Truly, God can exclaim in the inspired words of Jeremias: "I have loved you with an everlasting love" (Jeremias 31,3).

God's profusion of love toward creatures was not exhausted with natural creation. Two groups of His creatures were recipients of a yet greater demonstration of divine love. The angels and men were endowed with grace, with that special quality that inheres in their very spirits and gives them powers and a mode of life that is entirely above their natural powers. It makes angels and men very special friends of God, and even His children. It empowers them to know God, to love Him, and to enjoy Him as He is in Himself. It makes them heirs of heaven, entitling them to the right of a glorious life with God in His own home, where they can see Him face to face, clearly and directly, and love Him and enjoy Him with a proportionate love and joy. Of this St. John tells us:

Behold what manner of love the Father has bestowed upon us, that we should be called children of God; and such we are. . . . Beloved, now we are the children of God, and it has not yet appeared what we shall be. We know that, when he appears, we shall be like to him, for we shall see him just as he is. (1 John 3,1-3)

St. Paul assures us that the love we have for God in this life will continue forever in that face-to-face vision of God:

Charity never fails. . . . We see now through a mirror in an obscure manner, but then face to face. Now I know in part, but then I shall know even as I have been known. So there abide faith, hope and charity, these three; but the greatest of these is charity. (1 Corinthians 13,8-13)

That never-ending life of heavenly glory with the Triune God is the culmination of God's love toward each one of us. To repeat, God's ultimate and primary reason for creating us was the manifestation of His own glory; but He did will to create us, secondarily, for our glory, for our eternal and perfect happiness.

God willed to bestow all that profusion of love on men and angels through the mediation of His only-begotten Son, who would become man. As St. Paul states so concisely and beautifully in his letter to the Ephesians:

Blessed be the God and Father of our Lord Jesus Christ, who has blessed us with every spiritual blessing on high in Christ. Even as he chose us in him before the foundation of the world, that we should be holy and without blemish in his sight in love.

He predestined us to be adopted through Jesus Christ as his sons, according to the purpose of his will, unto the praise of the glory of his grace, with which he has favored us in his beloved Son. (Ephesians 1,3-6)

According to God's primal plan of creation, then, the Sacred Heart of Jesus was to be the center on which all God's outpouring of love would converge and from which it was to be radiated to all of us. And all of us would have to give glory to God and to love Him through Christ Jesus. The Sacred Heart of Jesus, too, is the final reason why God willed to bestow love on all others. But for God's immense outpouring of love on the Sacred Heart, there would have been no outpouring of love on anyone else. That is why St. Paul wrote to the Colossians:

He is the image of the invisible God, the firstborn of every creature. For in him were created all things in the heavens and on the earth, things visible and things invisible, whether Thrones or Dominations, or Principalities, or Powers. All things have been created through and unto him, and he is before all creatures, and in him all things hold together. (Colossians 1,15-17)

Christ is, then, not only the Mediator of all grace and glory, of divine love, for all angels and men; He is not only the end of all creation, but also the first in all creation according to God's mind. That is the full meaning of Paul's words to the Ephesians as well as to the Colossians just cited. He put this truth very concisely when he wrote to the Corinthians: "For all things are yours . . . and you are Christ's, and Christ is God's" (1 Corinthians 3,22-23). That is how Cardinal Pacelli (later Pope Pius XII) explained the matter in a beautiful sermon given to a group of pilgrims in Rome, May 28, 1937, while he was Cardinal Secretary of State for

Pope Pius XI. Having stated that Mary is the first of all creation and that this is the mind of the Church when she applies Proverbs 8,22-25 to her, he explains:

Wishing to create the world, at the beginning of time, in order to diffuse His love and to bring it about that there would exist other beings besides Himself who would be happy, God, before all things (if one may speak thus, according to our manner of seeing and acting successively)—God before all things cast His eyes upon Him who was to be their Head and King. He decreed that, to redeem the human race from the servitude of sin, the Word, born of the Father, consubstantial with the Father, should become incarnate and live among us. Here is the Masterpiece of God, the most excellent of His works. Regardless of what the date and the circumstances of His manifestation in time would be, it is certainly what He willed before all other things, and in view of which He made all other things (Colossians 1,15-17).

However, since He wished that this unique object of His good pleasure be born of a woman, He cast upon you, O Mary, a glance most sweet, and predestined you to be His Mother. Eternally, the material world appeared to Him as the palace of Christ, our Head; the angels and men as His servants; Christ Himself as the Son and the royal Prince; and you, O Virgin, as the most worthy Mother of His Son, the Mother of God. (Sermon on the Seventieth Anniversary of the Association of Our Lady of a Happy Death, May 28, 1937).[1]

Christ, then, is the recipient of the most lavish outpouring of God's love. He is the greatest Good in all creation. He, on His part, can give to God a return of love that is of infinite value, because He is the Son of God with a human nature. And because He is our Brother and our Mediator and our final end, we can share in His return of love for God. How good God was in granting us this privilege! Really, God is love!

God's goodness and love toward His creatures was truly marvellous. But what ingratitude on the part of some of His creatures! Some of the angels rejected God's love. They refused to serve Christ as King. They were cast from God's friendship forever because that is what they willed.

Man, too, sinned against God. But, oh, what unspeakable love of God! God had pity on man and in spite of man's offense, He willed to send His Son, Jesus Christ, as Redeemer. "God so loved the world," writes John, "that he gave his only-begotten Son, that those who believe in him may not perish, but may have life everlasting" (John 3,16). That is why St. Paul can add in his letter to the Ephesians:

In him we have redemption through his blood, the remission of sins, according to the riches of his grace. This grace has abounded beyond measure in us in all wisdom and prudence, so that he may make known to us the mystery of his will according to his good pleasure. And this his good pleasure he proposed in him to be dispensed in the fullness of the times: to re-establish all things in Christ, both those in the heavens and those on the earth. (Ephesians 1,7-10)

And to the Colossians he writes:

Again, he is the head of his body, the Church; he who is the beginning, the firstborn from the dead, that in all things he may have the first place. For it has pleased God the Father that in him all his fullness should dwell, and that through him he should reconcile to himself all things, whether on the earth or in the heavens, making peace through the blood of his cross. (Colossians 1,18-20)

And so it was that Christ Jesus came on this earth, lived here, suffered and died for us sinners that we might again enjoy the friendship and love of His Father on earth and forever in heaven.

That Christ loved us immensely is a historic fact, attested so abundantly in Sacred Scripture that there can be no doubt about it. Jesus described Himself as the Good Shepherd who lays down his life for the sheep (John 10,11.14). And He presented Himself as model when He said to the disciples: "Greater love than this no man has than that he lay down his life for a friend" (John 15,13). Christ's very Heart of love was pierced out of love for us.

The great St. Paul, who had a very tangible experience of God's love tells us:

> But God, who is rich in mercy, by reason of his very great love wherewith he has loved us even when we were dead by reason of our sins, brought us to life together with Christ (by grace you have been saved) and raised us up together, and seated us together in heaven in Christ Jesus, that he might show in the ages to come the overflowing riches of his grace in kindness towards us in Christ Jesus. (Ephesians 2,5-6).

We can all exclaim with Paul: "He loved me and gave himself up for me" (Galatians 2,20).

God showers His love on us through Christ, likewise by having established His one true, holy and universal Church as the ordinary means for us to receive supernatural life and to work out our salvation. That is why, in His supreme goodness, He endowed His Church with His own infallible authority that we might always live in peace and security that come from possessing the truth. That is why He entrusted to the Church the renewal of His sacrifice on the Cross that we might have an easy and visible means of applying the fruits of the redemption to ourselves. That is why He gave to the Church all the Sacraments, those visible channels of grace and divine friendship.

Our Divine Savior demonstrates His love toward us by incorporating us into His Mystical Body, the Church, through Baptism, by strengthening us as true soldiers of His through Confirmation, by forgiving us our offenses over and over again. Most of all, however, He manifests His love for us in the Sacrament of His love, Holy Communion, whereby He unites Himself with us in a most intimate manner and helps us to grow in the life of charity, in closer union with Himself and all members of His Mystical Body.

In that setting of Divine Love we must necessarily fit the picture of the mystery of love of men for God.

CHAPTER TWO

The Mystery of Man's Love for God

WE HAVE SHOWN THAT GOD CREATED US, ULTIMATELY AND primarily, that we might give glory to Him, but secondarily that we might receive glory from Him and be eternally happy with Him. That ultimate end of man, primary and secondary, must be the measure of man. Everything that might be said of man and the reasons for his existence must be measured in final analysis by that twofold purpose.

Man's existence in this world must, then, be gauged by the fact that he is destined for a life of perfect happiness with God after death. Knowledge, love and service of God in this world, and everything this implies and demands, must be the stepping stone to the happiness of loving God forever. The present life must be a preparation for the future life. Since the future life is to be a life of loving God perfectly in return for His love of us, the present life too must be a life of love for God. Our Catechism expresses that very succinctly: "God made man to know Him, to love Him, and to serve Him in this life, and to be happy with Him forever in the next." Knowledge of God is the prerequisite for loving God; joy is the necessary consequence; service is the condition. Love for God is, therefore, the essence of the purpose of man's creation. How could it be otherwise since God is the God of love! The mystery of God's love for man must be counterbalanced and completed by the mystery of man's love for God.

To achieve that end God gave man an immortal soul endowed with the faculty of knowing the truth and loving the good and enjoying both the truth and the good. These faculties God strengthened beyond their natural capacities by grace, specifically by the virtues of faith, love and hope. These faculties, elevated by grace, are the most important, by which man is to strive for holiness on earth and happiness in heaven, by which man is to fulfill the mystery of love.

Those spiritual faculties are not the only ones man has received from the Creator. Man has been given a body as an instrument of the immortal soul. Through it he is capable of sentient life—of sight, hearing, smell, taste, touch. With these sentient powers man functions in a visible, material world. Moreover, the soul gives to the body vegetative life, by which the body continues to preserve itself and to grow to maturity.

All these faculties of man, the intellectual, the sentient, the vegetative, must cooperate in preparing man to enjoy an eternal happiness hereafter. And by God's generous love the body will share in that eternal, happy life of the immortal soul.

Man, then, as an individual creature must strive to perfect himself, especially in love, and thus to attain everlasting happiness. But man is also a social being. He must live in a society of men like himself. He cannot work toward his eternal happiness entirely independently of other men. In various ways he must help others toward the possession of eternal happiness in loving God.

For our purpose we must explain that there are two basic ways in which men must cooperate with fellow men toward helping each other to realize an eternal happiness of love with God. The first way is to work with God in giving existence to other men, in begetting them to a natural life. By special design God did not create all men in the beginning of time, as He did all the angels. He created only one pair, Adam and Eve. To them, and through them to all men, He gave the power to cooperate with Himself in peopling the world and heaven. For that purpose He made one a male and the other a female, each with a special but different power for cooperating with the other, and with Himself, the Creator of the soul, in procreating children.

This power of generation is a sharing in God's omnipotent creative power. In itself it is a very good thing, physically and morally, partaking as it does of the creative power of the all-holy God. It is good in its immediate purpose and in its ultimate purpose. In its immediate purpose of bringing people into the world so they may share in God's knowledge and love and happiness and do service to Him; in its ultimate purpose of making it possible for them to live a glorious life forever with God and each other. Or, in other words, the power of sex is a great boon, inasmuch as it permits man to cooperate with God in creating members for the Mystical Body of Christ on earth, who will be able to perfect themselves and then continue to live forever as members of the glorified Mystical Body of Christ in heaven. God has conferred a singular dignity on man and woman and imposed on them also a tremendous duty.

The use of the power of sex by man and woman tends to an immortal being, because God bound Himself, by His own laws, so that when man and woman together use this power of procreation and a new cell-life results, God creates an immortal soul and unites it with that tiny cell-life in the womb of the woman. The result is an immortal being who needs not only to grow to maturity and to be given birth, but to be cared for a long time after birth. He needs physical and spiritual care. He must be fed and clothed and sheltered; he must be educated not only for a temporal and material existence, but for a spiritual and eternal life. For all this the child has the continued need of father and mother. God, the all-wise Creator, therefore, so ordained and decreed—and He wrote the decree in the heart of every man and woman, as well as on the stone slabs of Moses—that among human beings the power of sex may be used lawfully only by a man and a woman who are united by a valid contract in a permanent state of life, called marriage, for the specific primary purpose of rearing children. Every other use of that sacred power He forbade and must forbid as unlawful. True, for those who are so united in lawful wedlock the power of sex may be also an expression of mutual love and legitimate pleasure; but only for such.

In view of all this, man and woman alike need to practice a special virtue, whereby the use of the sacred function of sex is controlled according to God's laws. One cannot object that man has the power and can use it according to his pleasure. The simple fact that man has a power gives him no right to use it as he pleases. Faculties that God has given to man may be used only for furthering the achievement of man's final end; not for hindering that achievement. Man may not use his power of knowing to deny God, or his power of loving to hate God. He may not abuse his power of sentient appetite by stuffing himself with food or drink, or by starving himself. He must control this power according to the dictates of right reason by the virtue of temperance, so that it will aid him to attain his ultimate end. In the same way he must control the power of sex according to the dictates of right reason by the virtue of chastity.

God Himself instituted the vocation and state of matrimony by uniting Adam and Eve in holy wedlock and giving them the command to have children. "Be fruitful and multiply," He told them; "fill the earth and subdue it" (Genesis 1,28). He even indicated the matrimonial union of man and wife by forming Eve somehow from Adam.

The Lord God cast the man into a deep sleep and, while he slept, took one of his ribs and closed up its place with flesh. And the rib which the Lord God took from the man, he made into a woman, and brought her to him. Then the man said, 'She now is bone of my bone, and flesh of my flesh; she shall be called Woman, for from man she has been taken.' For this reason a man leaves his father and mother, and clings to his wife, and the two become one flesh. (Genesis 2,21-24)

In reference to this St. Paul wrote: "This [union of husband and wife] is a great mystery—I mean in reference to Christ and to the Church" (Ephesians 5,32). From the very beginning God intended the sacred matrimonial union to be a symbol of the union between Christ and His Church. And this symbolism reached its perfection when Christ raised the matrimonial union to the state of a sacrament. This shows the close relation between marriage and the Mystical Body, inasmuch as marriage is ultimately instituted for the perfection of the Mystical Body of Christ; and both tend to the heavenly glory of men. By the primary end of their vocation, therefore, husband and wife cooperate in realizing the mystery of divine love.

God commanded Adam and Eve to make use of their power of sex for the procreation of children because they were the first and only pair in existence then. It was necessary for them to make use of their privileged power to get the human family started. For them this was a personal command. For all their descendants it was not personal. It was given, in the persons of Adam and Eve, to the entire human race; it does not bind every individual of the human race personally. It binds the race as a whole, inasmuch as there must always be some—and there will always be a sufficient number—who will have to marry and rear children, and keep the race not only from dying out but also growing. Individuals, therefore, do not have the personal obligation of getting married and of making use of the power of sex. They may remain single for a lifetime, if there are solid reasons for doing so. But from what is said above, it is clear that one who does remain single is bound to the observance of perfect chastity.

That leads us to the second basic way for helping fellow men to attain the eternal happiness of love with God, namely, to aid them to know about God and His means of salvation, and to live according to this knowledge. In keeping with the ideas of Sacred Scripture we can speak of this as begetting children for a spiritual, supernatural life, as being father and mother to fellow men in regard to the supernatural life to which they are destined.

Parents are by their office bound to care for the spiritual life of their children, to beget them to a supernatural as well as a natural life. Others may take a special interest in the spiritual upbringing and well-being of fellow men. To devote oneself more directly and completely to the salvation of fellow men, to teaching, guiding and sanctifying members of the Mystical Body of Christ, to helping them realize their essential and ultimate purpose in life, to aiding them in fulfilling the mystery of God's love is a very solid reason for remaining single and living in perfect chastity, instead of getting married and procreating children for a natural life.

In the true Church of Christ there are official ministers

for the apostolate of saving souls. In fact, Christ has set them apart from the rest of the members by a very special sacrament, Holy Orders, in order to give them the required power for their ministry and the grace for fruitfully exercising that power. To remain single and to live in perfect chastity is for these ministers of Christ a great asset. It frees them from temporal cares to give themselves unreservedly to the care of souls. It frees them from worldly interests to devote themselves wholeheartedly to loving God. It makes them very like Christ, the virginal eternal High Priest. These reasons more than justify their renouncing marriage and living in perfect chastity. This vocation of the virginal priesthood tends in a pre-eminent way toward the fulfillment of the mystery of divine love.

There are other groups in the Church of Christ that dedicate themselves to a service of Christ and His Church in perfect chastity. There are those who consecrate themselves to God either in religious community life or in secular institutes by the three vows of poverty, chastity and obedience. They do so first for the purpose of making their own spiritual life on earth and their eternal salvation in heaven more secure and more perfect. They do so secondly for the purpose of being able to help others more wholeheartedly and more completely to save their souls. Detachment from worldly pleasures and temporal interests by a life of perfect chastity, as well as by the observance of poverty and obedience, frees a person for complete devotion to God's service in contemplation or in the apostolate of saving others through a variety of ministrations. These, too, are sufficient reasons for renouncing marriage and practicing perfect chastity. This vocation contributes in an eminent way to the fulfillment of the mystery of divine love.

There is another group of men and women that live single

lives in perfect chastity. They do so in the world, without belonging to a religious society or even a secular institute. We aim to show the lawfulness and excellence of this vocation of single perfect chastity in the world as a fulfilling of the mystery of divine love.

CHAPTER THREE

The Single Vocation in the World

THERE HAVE ALWAYS BEEN ENEMIES OUTSIDE THE CHURCH who have attacked the celibacy of the clergy and denounced the perfect chastity of religious. With the defense of such single people we are not concerned directly, though much of what we say about chastity for the single in the world holds equally for the priests and religious. Directly we are concerned with the vocation of men and women in the world who wish to live a life of perfect chastity in the single state. The legitimacy of this vocation has been attacked by those outside the Church. Even some Catholics seem to have had inaccurate, incomplete, and disparaging ideas on the matter.

We aim, therefore, to prove that it is lawful for people to remain in the world and live a single life of perfect chastity for the sublime purpose of attaining their primary end in life more easily and securely, thereby achieving a more complete and perfect personality, and ultimately for the purpose of obtaining a more perfect life of glory in heaven—all this for the greater honor and glory of Christ and God.

That such perfect chastity is quite legitimate is clear,

first, from the fact that no one of less authority than Christ counselled it. He invited all those who feel capable of living that life to accept it when He said: "And there are eunuchs who have made themselves so for the kingdom of heaven's sake. Let him accept it who can" (Matthew 19,12). This invitation of Christ is general, it is not limited to priests or religious. His invitation implies that the vocation is difficult, but that it can be chosen freely by anyone who feels he can live it. And the reason He assigned for such a life is "for the kingdom of heaven's sake." Anyone may choose it for that reason, is Christ's meaning; not merely those who for various reasons are barred from entering other vocations.

St. Paul, too, is warrant for the lawfulness of such a vocation of virginal love in the world. In his long and beautiful seventh chapter to the Corinthians about virginity and married life, he argues not only that this is a lawful vocation but that it is more perfect than the vocation of married life.

For I would that you all were as I myself; but each one has his own gift from God, one in this way, and another in that. But I say to the unmarried and to widows, it is good for them if they so remain, even as I. (I Corinthians 7,7-8)

Later he explains:

He who is unmarried is concerned about the things of the Lord, how he may please God. Whereas he who is married is concerned about the things of the world, how he may please his wife; and he is divided. And the unmarried woman, and the virgin, thinks about the things of the Lord, that she may be holy in body and in spirit. Whereas she who is married thinks about the things of the world, how she may please her husband. Now this I say for your benefit, not to put a halter upon you, but to promote what is proper, and to make it possible for you to pray to the Lord without distraction. (1 Corinthians 7,32-35)

And he concludes:

But she will be more blessed, in my judgment, if she remains as she is [namely, a virgin]. And I think that I also have the spirit of God. (1 Corinthians 7,40)

St. Paul was speaking directly of women virgins, but his thoughts have equal force for men who live in perfect chastity. That is evident from the fact that he proposes himself as a model even for the women virgins. In view of that clear teaching of Christ and St. Paul, it is not surprising that Holy Mother Church, who is herself the virginal Spouse of Christ, approved of this vocation from the very beginning, and protected it against the attacks of heretics and immoral persons. By her infallible authority she has declared that this vocation is better, in itself, than that of the married. The Council of Trent made this statement: "If anyone says that the conjugal state is to be preferred to the state of virginity or celibacy, and that it is not better and more blessed to remain in virginity or celibacy than to enter matrimony, let him be condemned. (Session 24, canon 10).[2] Though the Council had religious and priests more in mind, its canon was meant also for men and women who live a life of virginity in the world.

In our own day Pope Pius XII, in a discourse on the vocation of woman in the modern world, praised the thousands who through the twenty centuries of the Church's history have followed Christ's counsel and freely renounced marriage to consecrate their services to humanity by prayer and penance, by every kind of work of charity toward children, the ignorant, the sick, the dying. These remarks of the Pope do not refer exclusively to priests and religious. He praised those, too, who freely renounced marriage for the sake of a life of contemplation, of sacrifice and of charity.

In regard to these, he said, one immediately thinks of a "vocation"; namely, that they have a true calling for that life from God. Then, to encourage those who because of circumstances of war had to remain unmarried, he added that they, too, have a "vocation," a call from God for their single lives, and their lives need not be useless for society. (Discourse, Oct. 21, 1945)[3]

It would be quite erroneous to think that the Pope did not recommend a single life in the world except for those who were forced to remain unmarried. Such a deduction, as our analysis of the whole section shows, would be utterly false. The Pope would never make such a primitive error in so important a matter of Christian living. He was speaking of a fact due to war conditions. He was not laying down an exclusive principle. In fact, just before that he spoke of those who voluntarily choose such a vocation. For them it is a "vocation" without doubt. But it can be a "vocation," he wished to explain, also for those who remain unmarried by force of circumstances.

Already prior to that discourse, on Holy Saturday, 1943, in an allocution to the Italian girls of Catholic Action,[4] the Pope praised "the sons and daughters in the earliest Church, who freely renounced earthly nuptials for the love of Christ, consecrated all their powers to the duties of caring for souls, of Christian education, of charity, of foreign missions." He then spoke of those who were even martyred for their faith and purity. Only later does he mention religious. Those referred to earlier evidently include lay people who lived in perfect chastity, as is clear too from his speaking of the "earliest Church," when there were no religious in the strict sense.

But the Holy Father gave a more solemn approval to the single life in the world in his encyclical *On Holy Virginity*, March 25, 1954. This document deals generally with virginity as lived by priests and religious, but many points apply equally to lay people who live in perfect chastity. In one passage in particular he speaks expressly of lay people:

> But while such perfect chastity is the object of one of the three vows, of which the religious state consists, and while it is required of the clergy of the Latin Church in major Orders, and is demanded from the members of secular institutes; it, nevertheless, flourishes also among not a few who belong entirely to the laity. For there are men and women who are not established in a public state of perfection, and still they abstain entirely from matrimony and the carnal pleasures by virtue of a resolve or a private vow, in order that they may more freely serve their fellow men and that they may unite their souls more easily and closely with God.[5]

We have here an authoritative as well as an express approval of the single vocation even for those who are not forced into it but who choose it freely.

Virginal chastity in the world has, through the centuries, received at least implicit approval from the Vicars of Christ by the fact that they have beatified and canonized many men and women who lived this form of life. They have presented them to the whole world as models to be imitated.

The high esteem in which this calling was held in the life of the Church will be illustrated in a later chapter on the bridal concept of this life and in a chapter on the history of virginal life in the Church.

One can easily demonstrate how such a vocation is in complete accord with right reason. Let us begin with those who for some cause are hindered from choosing the married state. There are many people of both sexes who because of special circumstances of health or character or temporal needs must remain single. Many men and women are not meant for the priesthood or for the religious life, or even for secular institutes, either because of unfitness through sickness or a peculiar character, or because of circumstances which necessitate their staying at home to support aged parents or orphaned brothers or sisters, or because there was no opportunity for marriage, or because for reasons of study or a career they passed by opportunities of marriage until it was too late. Those that are unfit for the priesthood or convent life should not be pushed into married life if they are not qualified for that either. Because of character or sickness they might be misfits even in the married state. A mother, in particular, is often at fault in wanting to marry off her daughter at any cost after she could not take the convent life. To marry one off just so he or she will not be an old bachelor or an old maid is erroneous theology and foolish reasoning. Celibacy and virginity are not a calamity to be avoided at any price.

It was precisely for those who after the late war had no opportunity of marriage that Pope Pius XII, as we saw, said their lives need not be useless. They too have a vocation if, in their singleness, they devote themselves to social works and, of course, observe perfect chastity. They need not be mere reluctant bachelors or spinsters. True, if such had been fit or had had the opportunity for marriage, they would have chosen this vocation; but since that is out of reach for them, they should consider it God's will that they live a single life in the world devoted to works of charity. They must live in perfect chastity in any case; they might as well get the most out of it for themselves and mankind by their charitable services.

That such a vocation is pleasing to God and willed by Him is clear, or else He could never permit situations to arise in which one is forced to remain single. Perhaps it was in the design of Divine Providence to permit the late war and its aftermath that deprived many of the opportunity of marriage in order to teach the modern world that a single life in perfect chastity is according to His will and can be most valuable for humanity.

We must, however, establish that this vocation of perpetual perfect chastity in the world is legitimate even for those who are not forced to remain in it, even for those who would be qualified for one of the other vocations but who wish to choose this form of life as more suited to their inclinations and loves. Such a vocation would be unlawful only if all men and women were obliged to be priests and/or religious or to get married. That not all are capable of being, much less obliged to be, priests or religious needs no proof. And we showed above that God's command to Adam and Eve to make use of the marriage rights binds the whole race as such, to the extent that some always must marry and have children for the continuance of the race. But there never will be any danger that too many will forego marriage or the having of children so that the race would become extinct. The instinct of fatherhood and motherhood was planted too deeply in the hearts of men and women by the Creator Himself. Those, comparatively few, who wish to forego marriage will in no way jeopardize the preservation of the race. They are quite free to choose the single life of perfect chastity.

Nor is the experience of sexual intercourse necessary for full realization of one's personality, for complete self-realization, inasmuch as the two sexes are meant to complement each other, as some moderns argue. The plain fact is that there are many married people who do not fully realize their personality in spite of plentiful enjoyment of sexual relations. The reason is not far to seek. Sexual pleasure is not the most important end of man's existence, nor a necessary means toward the ultimate end of man's existence. The moderns who are obsessed by the importance of sex are heretics or materialists or both. They fail to grasp the nature of sex and marriage and the place of these in the harmonious nature of man and of human society; they fail to understand the nature and purpose of man as such. They fail to realize that sex is only one faculty in man; not the most important one by any means, and one that need not be used at all without jeopardizing man's reaching his final end in life perfectly.

Man was created with a spiritual soul and endowed with the faculties of intellect and will, of understanding and love. When these two faculties do not achieve the object that alone can make them perfectly happy, then a man's personality is not complete. Man, in other words, is not striving for perfect happiness and a complete personality if he excludes God from his knowledge and love. Without God there is a void in man's soul; the essential object of his knowledge and love is lacking. Nothing else can fill that void. Whoever, therefore, attains to the knowledge and love of God, and lives accordingly, realizes his essential personality to the full.

Anent this the Holy Father wrote:

More recently, however, sad of soul We have condemned the opinion of those who went so far as to assert that marriage is the one thing that can secure the natural development of the human personality and its due perfection. There are, namely, those who claim that divine grace, which is conferred by the sacrament of matrimony *ex opere operato,* makes the use of matrimony so holy that it becomes a more efficacious instrument for uniting single souls with God than virginity itself, since Christian matrimony, not virginity, is a sacrament. This doctrine We denounce as false and harmful. (*On Holy Virginity,* p. 175 f.)

So not even the sacramental state of matrimony is more suited for perfecting human personality than the solitary state of virginity.

Man has, it is true, been endowed with a body that has sentient and vegetative faculties. These may not be mutilated, and they must be used and controlled in such a way that they do not hinder the essential end of man as an individual and as a social being. At times one may forego their use, in order to attain the essential end more easily and securely. Now among the faculties of the body is sex. It is not an essential faculty at all as far as the human person is concerned. In fact, it was not given for personal perfection; it was given for the continuance of the race. Its primary purpose is not personal, but social.

Those moderns who measure life in terms of sex are still blatantly propagating the falsehood that perfect chastity is harmful to the physical and nervous health of a person, and that, on the other hand, the use of sex powers promotes health. Neither assertion is true; both are utterly false. The non-use of sex is not only not harmful physically and psychically, but is a form of temperance quite conducive to health, especially of the nervous system, that is, in those who freely choose such a life and live it cheerfully. In those who regret being shackled by perfect chastity it can be frustrating.

In regard to the above error the Holy Father has this to say:

And first of all, it is undoubtedly not in keeping with the common opinion of upright men (for which the Church has always had high regard) to consider the natural instinct of sex as the more important and greater tendency of a human being, and to conclude from this that man cannot inhibit this appetite during his entire lifetime without the grave danger of ruining the health of his body, and especially the nerves, and consequently, throwing his human personality out of balance. (*On Holy Virginity*, p. 174 f.)

That clears the way for us to present the two positive reasons that make the choice of this form of life quite lawful. Since we shall treat each in a separate chapter, we shall mention them at this time only briefly. Virginal love, we said, is not an impediment to the full realization of one's personality. It is not only no hindrance to the fullest attainment of one's final end, but it promotes that attainment as nothing else can. It not only does not hinder the realization of a perfect personality; it is, very positively, the completion, the sublimation, the perfection of human personality. The reason is this: perfect chastity makes it possible for man and woman to possess most fully and completely in this world the God who alone can be the fully satisfying object of man's essential faculties, which otherwise is possible only in the heavenly life. God and Christ must be loved above all else, and everyone and everything must be loved in and through Christ and God. Precisely in perfect chastity is this twofold love possible to the highest degree in this world. In perfect chastity man and woman can love God with an undivided love. They are, then, not bachelors and spinsters because they love so little; they are virginal spouses of Christ because they love so much, so ardently, that no creature can fully satisfy their longing for loving and being loved. They are, in short, on fire with love for God. This is the essence of the mystery of love for the single in the world.

The perfection of one's own personality is the primary reason for choosing the life of perfect chastity. It is not the only reason. This vocation is not a selfish one. True, the adversaries object that people who deliberately remain single in the world are selfish in not marrying and rearing children who could be a boon to society. That is missing the point entirely. Those who forego marriage and practice perfect chastity do so precisely because, besides securing their own salvation, they can be a great blessing to the Church and society at large. Precisely because such single men and women are so beneficial to the Church and are such a power for the Church's apostolate do the heretics oppose them and persecute them. The persecutors of the Church of all times are the greatest witnesses to the social blessing that perfect chastity has been, is, and will be.

Nor is the fact of their being persecuted an argument that the vocation is not healthy for society. Christ was the one who foretold that His Church, His virginal Spouse, would be persecuted. But she is persecuted only inasmuch as her members are persecuted, not merely in her hierarchical members, in bishops and priests, but also, and very much so, in her virginal lay members. Precisely these have produced the most beautiful flowers of purity and martyrdom in the early Church, as for example, St. Agnes and St. Agatha. If, then, the virginal lovers of Christ are persecuted so much, that is a clear and irrefutable argument that they are very much a part of the true Church of Christ, their Virgin Mother and Model. They are, in this point, very much like Christ Himself.

Lastly, such a vocation to virginal love in the world will be no detriment to vocations to the priesthood or to the religious life. That needs no proof as far as those are concerned who remain of necessity unmarried, because these should not or cannot choose the priestly or religious vocation. But it is true even in regard to those who freely choose to be virgins in the world, though they might have the qualifications for other vocations. The God who grants the vocations to the virgins in the world will see to it that there will always be sufficient vocations in the other states of life.

Such virginal souls will themselves be instrumental in leading many others to the altar or into the convent. In fact, some may eventually choose such a vocation themselves precisely because they prepared for it by the virginal life they lived in the world. One may encourage such as are thinking about perfect chastity in the world to consider the priestly or the religious vocation, especially in view of the great shortage in these vocations. But these latter vocations must be chosen freely. If one still thinks that one can fulfill God's will by a single life in the world, one is free to choose that vocation. To do so is not to have a low esteem of the priesthood or of the religious life. Just as to praise and foster vocations to the single life in the world is not a belittling of the priesthood or of the religious life. To esteem silver is not to despise gold; to extol clarinets is not to denounce violins; to praise violets is not to damn roses.

Chapter Four

Spiritual Nuptials through Perfect Chastity

Chastity for the single is necessarily a negative virtue; it is abstinence from the use of a faculty, from the use and enjoyment of sex. But it is not merely negative, especially when it is deliberately chosen and willed for the more perfect end of undivided love for Christ. It has then a preeminently positive value: the love of and union with Christ. Chastity, perfect and perpetual, is not merely a negation, an inhibition of powers, a non-exercise of sex, a fighting against temptations. It is something quite positive. It is as positive as love of Christ, which in fact makes it quite reasonable, quite intelligible. It does not make a person, or suppose that a person is, emotionless, or even without the passion of sex. Such a person would be abnormal. A chaste person is essentially normal in his passions and emotions. Virginal chastity is full of love, full of the spiritual love of Christ.

With this idea we enter into the realm of the mystic. Virginal love is mystical union with Christ, which results in being loved, protected, consoled, rejoiced by Christ. It is in no sense the mere ascetical endurance of a passionless existence. In its positive aspect especially, it is far superior to married love. Even for married people the ultimate end of their human love must be the mystic love of Christ. And often when marriage, from the point of human love, fails to satisfy, the married must seek spiritual satisfaction in supernatural love and mystic union with Christ.

Virginal love is as positive, too, as a consecration. The gold chalice with which a priest celebrates the Holy Eucharist may be used for no other purpose than consecrating the Precious Blood of Christ. The chalice was made sacred for that purpose alone; it was set aside exclusively for that use. That is certainly a pre-eminently positive use and purpose. Through dedicated virginity or perfect chastity, in like manner, one sets aside as sacred to Christ the power of sex, in order that one's entire person may be devoted to Christ's service and love more completely. That is assuredly something positive. We must note, however, that (every simile limps) the chalice which is consecrated for only the one purpose is itself used for that purpose, whereas in perfect chastity it is not the power of sex itself that is used. The power of sex is consecrated to Christ not to be used at all, in order that another faculty, that of spiritual love, may be more completely devoted to Christ and used to its fullest capacity.

Virginal love is as positive, again, as the Eucharistic Sacrifice itself. It is a sacrificing of the power of sex, in order that the power of love might be exercised in a more sublime and perfect fashion. It is the perfect communion of Christ with the soul through undivided love.

Consecrated chastity is, finally, as positive as marriage. It is a marriage, spiritual nuptials with Christ. This idea has been sacred in the Church from the earliest times. It is so important and attractive that we shall dwell on it at length.

Every Christian soul is a bride of Christ. Why do we use this figure of speech? We use it because of the similarity between the nuptial relation of husband and wife and the spiritual relation of Christ and the soul, particularly in regard to the intimate and undivided love. Nuptial love is the deepest, the noblest and the most intimate of human loves. Let us remark here that whatever we say about Christ as spouse of the soul and of virgins is true of God as spouse too. For brevity's sake we will ordinarily not express both. We must note, too, that with the advent of Christ into the spiritual life of man, man's nuptial relation cannot be merely to God, it must also be to Christ. So we usually mention only Christ, implying, however, that what is said of Christ is true also of the Triune God.

We shall be able to appreciate the excellence of the spiritual nuptials more if we make a more detailed comparison with the marriage contract and state. In the latter the following points are present. There is a bilateral contract giving complete right over one's body for the primary purpose of procreation of children, and for the secondary purpose of mutual love of spouse and lawful expression of sexual pleasure. Consequent upon that contract there is a moral union that is undivided and perpetual, and which calls for loyalty and love.

The soul and Christ make a kind of bilateral contract at the moment of justification. In this contract there is complete surrender of the soul to Christ and of Christ to the soul. Christ, because of His infinite perfection, can belong completely to more than one soul, to millions in fact. Further, in these spiritual nuptials the mutual surrender has as its primary purpose mutual love. In other words, the secondary purpose of marriage, mutual love, becomes the primary purpose in the spiritual nuptials. Spiritual nuptials—we shall have occasion to explain—are not fruitless. They are an aid for rearing children of God for heaven. The primary purpose of marriage has, then, some kind of parallel also in the spiritual nuptials, though as secondary purpose. But the primary purpose of mutual love in the spiritual nuptials far surpasses in excellence the love of married people for each other. As to the second part of our comparison with marriage, the union, the love-union established by grace between Christ and the soul is very intimate and is of itself permanent and undivided. The mystic concept, therefore, of spiritual nuptials for the justified soul is quite legitimate.

There is a basis in Sacred Scripture for considering the sanctified soul a spouse of Christ. Already in Old Testament times it was customary to regard the relation of the Chosen Nation of Israel to God as that of bride to spouse. See Isaias 54,1; Ezechiel 16,6-63; Osee 1-3; Jeremias 2,2; Canticle. But even in the Old Testament it was especially the New Israel, the Church which the Messias would bring into being, that was looked upon as the bride of the Messias; see Psalm 44 and the Canticle.

This bridal union between Christ and the Church is beautifully described by St. Paul as a fact achieved:

Husbands love your wives, just as Christ also loved the Church, and delivered himself up for her, that he might sanctify her, cleansing her in the bath of water by means of the word; in order that he might present to himself the Church in all her glory, not having spot or wrinkle or any such thing, but that she might be holy and without blemish. Even thus ought husbands also to love their wives as their own bodies. He who loves his own wife, loves himself. For no one ever hated his own flesh: on the contrary, he nourishes and cherishes it, as Christ also does the Church, because we are members of his body, made from his flesh and from his bones: 'For this reason a man shall leave his father and mother, and shall cleave to his wife; and the two shall become one flesh' (Genesis 2,24). This is a great mystery—I mean in reference to Christ and to the Church. (Ephesians 5,25-32)

St. John, too, in his visions sees the Church as the heavenly bride of Christ:

> Let us be glad and rejoice, and give glory to him;
> for the marriage of the Lamb has come,
> and his spouse has prepared herself.
> And she has been permitted to clothe herself
> in fine linen, shining, bright.
> For the fine linen is the just deeds of the saints.
> (Apocalypse 19,7-8)

> And I saw the holy city, the New Jerusalem, coming down out of heaven, from God, made ready as a bride adorned for her husband. (Apocalypse 21,2)

In his first letter to the Corinthians, St. Paul explains: "I have betrothed you to one spouse, that I may present you as a chaste virgin to Christ" (11,2). Paul is thinking of the entire community at Corinth as the virgin spouse of Christ. But what is true of all the Christians at Corinth as a "church" is true of each member of that Church, since it cannot be true of the entire community except inasmuch as it is true of individual members, through whom alone the entire Church exists. What is true of the Corinthians is true of all Christians the world over: they are spiritual spouses of Christ.

We should like to note here, once and for all, that in the natural order of marriage, man is the active principle, woman the passive, physically and psychically. In the supernatural order of mystic nuptials Christ, the Bridegroom, is the active principle, and men, male and female, are the passive principle, because in relation to God all creatures are passive. Hence, whatever we say of spiritual nuptials and virginal love holds equally of men and women.

Every Christian soul is a spouse of Christ. That is true

in a fuller sense of a religious by virtue of profession. There is a more complete mutual surrender of the soul and all its faculties to Christ; there is a more intimate love; the union is more undivided and irrevocable. The perpetual vows, simple or solemn, make this state everlasting.

That a religious is in a special way the bride of Christ has been the common view in the Church for many centuries. Witness the ceremony of consecrating virgins, to which we shall refer frequently. Likewise, Christ teaches this truth clearly in revelations to some of His Saints. To St. Margaret Mary Alacoque, for instance, He said on her profession day: "Until now I have been only your Fiancé: I shall from now on be your Spouse." The Saints thought of themselves as spouses of Christ. St. Thérèse, for instance, in a letter of invitation to her sister for her profession, beautifully reveals how she thought of her profession day as a wedding day.

It is, however, through the free dedication of oneself by perpetual and perfect chastity that a person becomes the bride of Christ in the most complete sense. By the promise freely to live a life of perfect and perpetual chastity the parallels between spiritual nuptials and the marriage contract and state are verified in the fullest and sublimest sense.

There is, first, a most complete mutual surrender. No surrender of creature to Christ is more complete than this. True, by the vow of obedience the religious surrenders himself to Christ with his highest faculty, the will. But by perfect chastity a person surrenders to Christ the very powers that are surrendered in an earthly marriage, though not for the same purpose. In marriage the power of sex is surrendered primarily for the fruitfulness of children and only secondarily for mutual love and sexual pleasure. In the spiritual nuptials of perfect chastity the same power of sex is surrendered to Christ to be preserved intact forever by

His grace, primarily so that one can love Christ more intensely and more completely, but only secondarily so that one can devote oneself more wholeheartedly to spiritual fruitfulness, the salvation of souls. In spiritual nuptials, therefore, the power of sex is not realized at all. There is, however, a spiritualization of the whole person, including sex, so that one lives a kind of heavenly life, in which, namely, according to Christ's doctrine, there are no marriages. It is to be noted that through perfect chastity the highest faculty of man, the will, is not directly surrendered and dedicated to Christ; nevertheless, the surrender of the power of sex makes possible the most complete dedication of that highest faculty, for loving Christ, literally, with *all* one's heart.

The purpose of the contract of perfect chastity is a most intimate love of Christ. The result of the contract is an undivided and perpetual love-union. No other lover can have an equal share with Christ's love. Virginal love seals the heart of the lover for Christ alone. Christ can say of His chaste bride: "My sister, my spouse, is a garden enclosed, a garden enclosed, a fountain sealed up" (Canticle 4,12). Again, He can invite His virginal bride: "Put me as a seal upon your heart, as a seal upon your arm, for love is strong as death" (Canticle 8,6).

Since no human rival lover is admitted as spouse, the chaste bride can devote herself entirely to Christ's love. This love can, therefore, be most undivided, most intense, most profound. Since, too, it is in prayer that we express this love for Christ, it is in mystical prayer especially that the pure soul can find its delight, and to which it will devote itself. The self-surrender of a person in perfect chastity is an expression of the dearest love of the human heart for the Divine Heart of Jesus.

The chaste soul, so dedicated to the love of Christ, unites

itself with Christ in loving God in return for His immense love. The bride of Christ shares in His infinite love of God in a singular manner. She partakes of the mystery of divine love in a unique degree.

That this unique surrender through perfect chastity has for its purpose the undivided love of Christ was understood well by St. Paul. When he advised the state of virginity to the Corinthians, he expressed the idea that a married woman's attention is divided between her husband and God; a virgin's, on the contrary, is undivided: it can be given entirely to God. For that very reason virginity, he says, is the better gift (cf. 1 Corinthians 7,32-34). Through virginal purity, in other words, one can attain the ultimate purpose of his very existence more directly and perfectly. That is a purpose and a mode of life that is otherwise possible only in heaven, where marriages have no place. This is the reason why virginal life is spoken of as heavenly.

The love-union created by perpetual and perfect chastity is not only undivided in the fullest sense, it is also permanent; in fact, everlasting. In marriage an indissoluble bond is formed, but this state lasts only until the death of one of the spouses. In the spiritual nuptials there is an indissoluble bond that not even death can break. Death really makes that bond more permanent, and renders it infinitely sweeter by the beatific vision and the joyful love of the Divine Spouse. When one makes the promise of perfect chastity, one can say: "Until death do us more closely unite." Christ's counter-promise could be voiced in the words of the Prophet Osee: "I will betroth you to me forever" (Osee 2,19).

Our Holy Father has authoritatively approved this line of thought. First he shows how the Fathers of the Church viewed the consecrated virgin as Christ's bride:

The holy Fathers considered this bond of perfect chastity a kind of spiritual marriage, by which the soul is united with Christ. With that in mind some went so far as to compare with adultery the violation of the promised fidelity.[6] In keeping with that, St. Athanasius writes that the Catholic Church has the custom of calling brides of Christ those who possess the virtue of chastity.[7] St. Ambrose, too, when writing more precisely about the sacred virgin, has this: "A virgin is one who is wedded to God."[8] Moreover, as is clear from the writings of the same Doctor of Milan,[9] already from the fourth century the rite of consecration of virgins was very similar to the rite which the Church uses in our day for the blessing of a marriage. (*On Holy Virginity*, p. 166)

The Pope stresses, secondly, the love of Christ as the purpose of this espousal:

For the same reason the holy Fathers admonish the virgins that they love their divine Spouse more ardently than they would love the one to whom they might have been joined in wedlock, and that always, in thought and deed, they obey His will.[10] That is what St. Augustine writes to virgins: "Love Him [Christ] with all your heart, who is more beautiful than the sons of men; you are not pre-occupied, your heart is free from the bonds of marriage. . . . If, therefore, you would owe a great love to husbands, how much more ought you not to love Him for whose sake you wished not to have husbands? He should be fixed entirely in your hearts who was for your sake fixed to the cross.[11] That is in harmony, too, with the sentiments and intentions that the Church herself asks of the virgins on the day when they are solemnly consecrated to God, by inviting them to pronounce these words: "I have despised the kingdom of the world and every worldly ornament for the sake of the love of Our Lord Jesus Christ, whom I have seen, whom I have loved, in whom I have believed, of whom I have been very fond." So it is nothing else that sweetly compels the virgin to consecrate her body and soul entirely to the Divine Redeemer than love for Him. With that in mind St. Methodius, Bishop of Olympus, introduces the virgin as speaking these very beautiful words: "You Yourself, O Christ, are all things to me. For You, O Spouse, I keep myself pure, and holding a lighted lamp I go forth to meet You." [12] Indeed it is love for Christ that moves a virgin to seek refuge within convent walls and remain there perpetually, so that she can more freely and easily contemplate and love her heavenly Spouse. This love, too, strongly motivates her to devote herself till her dying day, with all her means, to works of mercy toward her neighbors. (*On Holy Virginity*, p. 166 f.)

In a later paragraph the Holy Father comes back to this idea of Christ's love as the motive of perfect chastity:

Here We think it opportune, Venerable Brothers, to give a fuller and more careful explanation why the love of Christ spurs generous souls on to abstain from marriage, and what mystic relations exist between virginity and the perfection of Christian charity. Already in Jesus Christ's statement, which we quoted above, it is suggested that such perfect abstinence from marriage frees men from its grave offices and duties. (*On Holy Virginity*, p. 168)

He explains at length, from St. Paul, 1 Corinthians 7, how perfect chastity is a liberation enabling one to be devoted to God by prayer and to fellow men by a more complete exercise of the works of mercy and of the apostolate of souls (*On Holy Virginity*, p. 168).

In a long paragraph, our Holy Father treats another reason for choosing a life of perfect and virginal chastity: likeness to Christ. One who loves Christ most intimately and perfectly wishes to be like Him in every respect, also in virginal purity, which, in turn, helps one to become more like Christ in all virtues.

As for the men "who were not defiled with women, for they are virgins," the Apostle John asserts: "These follow the Lamb wherever He goes" (Apocalypse 14,4). Let us, then, ponder on the exhortations that St. Augustine gives to all such virgins: "Follow the Lamb, because the body of the Lamb is indeed virginal. . . . Rightly do you follow Him with virginity of heart and body wherever He goes. For what does following mean if not imitating? Because Christ suffered for us and left us an example, as the Apostle Peter says, 'that we may follow in his steps' (1 Peter 2,21)." [13] Indeed, all these disciples and brides of Christ embraced the state of virginity, as St. Bonaventure says, "on account of likeness to Christ, the Spouse, for that state makes virgins like to Him." [14] For their ardent charity toward Christ could hardly be content with being united with Him by the bonds of the soul; it was necessary that this love prove itself by imitating His virtues, and in a peculiar manner by conforming to His way of life, which was spent entirely for the benefit and salvation of the human race. If priests, if religious men and women, if all those, finally, who have in any way dedicated themselves to the divine service, practice perfect chastity, the reason is certainly this, that their divine Master was a virgin until the end of His life. In keeping with that, St. Fulgentius exclaims: "This is the Only-begotten Son of God and the Only-begotten Son of the Virgin, the one Spouse of all consecrated virgins, the fruit, the glory, the reward of holy virginity, whom holy virginity brought forth in body, to whom holy virginity is wedded in spirit, by whom holy virginity is made fruitful, that it may remain intact, by whom it is adorned, that it may remain beautiful, by whom it is crowned, that it may have a glorious reign and everlasting." [15] (*On Holy Virginity*, p. 167 f.)

This ideal of espousal with Christ through perfect or virginal chastity is the theme song, as it were, of the beautiful ceremony for the blessing and consecration of virgins according to the Roman Pontifical. The ceremony has, in part, been revived in recent years in some convents of nuns.

Elements of it are embodied in the ceremonies for profession of Sisters. It will be instructive and inspiring to see how often the ideal of espousal is expressed in that ancient rite.

In the beginning the archpriest, in his invitation to the virgins, speaks of Christ as their Spouse: "Prudent virgins, prepare your lamps; behold the Spouse is coming; go out to meet Him." Then he addresses his petition to the Bishop, asking him whether he desires to "bless, consecrate, these virgins and espouse them to Our Lord Jesus Christ, the Son of the Most High God." The Bishop, in the very words of the archpriest's petition, answers that he does.

The spiritual nuptial relation is stressed in regard to four things: the dress, the veil, the ring, and the wreath. It was customary among some ancient peoples at weddings for the bride to remove the outer garment of her maidenhood and don the garment of an adult woman. There might be a relation between this custom and the donning of a new dress at the consecration of virgins. Note that at baptism the infant is clothed with a white dress, a nuptial dress. In the earlier ceremony for the Consecration of Virgins the dress was either white or dark according to different times and regions. In the present rite it must be of a dark color, no doubt to symbolize humility and detachment. The virgin could truly sing the words of Israel of old:

I will greatly rejoice in the Lord, and my soul shall be joyful in my God. For he has clothed me with the garments of salvation; and with the robe of justice he has covered me, as a bridegroom decked with a crown and as a bride adorned with her jewels. (Isaias 61:10)

That the dress was considered a symbol of the nuptials is brought out in the account of St. Euphrasia's consecration. Her mother prayed for her and said: "My dear child, do you wish to be clothed with this dress?" She replied:

Yes, dear Mother, because, as I know from Lady Abbess and as the Lady Sisters told me, the Lord Jesus Christ bestows this dress as a pledge on those who love Him.[16]

The veil was an integral part of the ceremony of Christian matrimony already in the fourth century. It was adopted from the ancient Roman custom, but at what time prior to the fourth century is unknown. The ancient Greeks and Etruscans used the veil at weddings. Among the Romans it was a symbol of conjugal love, of being married to one man only, of being veiled against every other suitor. In fact, the act of veiling or covering the bride, which in Latin is *obnubere*, gave to the Latin language the words *nubere* (to marry), *nuptiae* (marriage), and *nupta* (married woman).

The significance, then, of the veil at the wedding is that of undivided and exclusive love for one man. Consequently, when the veil was used for the consecration of a virgin, it was a symbol of the virgin not as a virgin, as single, but as a bride of Christ. That is why Pope St. Siricius could speak of "the virgin already veiled for Christ." [17] The veil became part of the official ceremony of consecration of virgins in the fourth century; but its use for virgins, as a sign of their being brides of Christ, existed already at the time of Tertullian. This writer of the early third century insists that a virgin wear the veil, so that she would no longer be sought after by men; and he notes that, if this would seem to be a deception, since she is actually not married, it is not altogether a deception, because she is married to Christ. In his treatise specifically on the veiling of virgins he writes:

Put on the panoply of modesty; surround yourself with the stockade of bashfulness; raise a wall for your sex—this should allow neither your own eyes to look out, nor others' eyes to look in. Wear the complete garb of a woman, that you may preserve the status of a virgin. Dissimulate somewhat your interior, in order to show the truth only to God, though you do not dissimulate a married woman, since you are wedded to Christ; to Him you have surrendered your body; to Him you have espoused your adulthood. Walk in accordance with the will of your Spouse. Christ it is who bids the espoused and the wives of others to veil themselves; and much more, indeed, His own spouses. (*On the Veiling of Virgins*, Ch. 16)[18]

Further, that the veil in this ceremony signifies nuptial relation is clearly contained in the prayers of the Consecration of Virgins. When the Bishop blesses the veil, he speaks, in the oration, of the virgins meriting "to enter the nuptials of everlasting happiness." When the veil is placed on the virgin's head, he prays:

Receive this sacred veil, by which you will be recognized as having despised the world, and as having subjected yourself perpetually as spouse of Christ Jesus, truthfully and humbly, and with every fibre of your heart.

The virgin herself sings: "He has placed a seal on my face, that I should admit no other lover." The chorus adds its chant: "Be espoused, beloved; come, the winter is passed, the dove sings, the blossoming vineyards give off their fragrance." The veil is, therefore, a symbol of the undivided love of the bride for the Spouse.

The ring is the sign of the espousal, of the love-union. It is a pledge of loyalty on the virgin's part, and a "sacrament" of gifts on Christ's part. He adorns the ring with diamonds of His grace. Often in the lives of saintly virgins,

Christ presented them with a special, mystic ring; e.g., St. Catherine of Siena, St. Rose of Lima. For the blessing of the ring the Bishop prays that those who wear these rings

. . . may be fortified by celestial strength, and so may guard faith entire and fidelity sincere; and may as Christ's spouses safeguard the resolve of virginity and persevere in perpetual chastity.

When the Bishop places the ring on the virgin's finger, he says:

I espouse you to Jesus Christ, the Son of the Most High Father, who should guard you inviolate. Receive, therefore, the ring of faith, the seal of the Holy Spirit, that you may be called the spouse of God, and that, if you serve Him faithfully, you may be crowned forever.

The virgin answers with this beautiful song:

I have been espoused to Him whom the angels serve, whose beauty the sun and the moon admire. My Lord Jesus Christ has made me a pledge with His ring, and has adorned me with a wreath as His spouse.

That leads us to the last point, the wreath. In the West, until the late Middle Ages, a wreath was placed on the head of the groom and the bride at the wedding ceremony. The wreath is the symbol of excellence, of dignity, of power, of glory and honor, of reward. It is a sign of the present dignity of Christ's spouse and a pledge of future glory and honor, even to the extent of receiving a special halo of happiness for perpetual chastity. At the beginning of the blessing of the wreath, the Bishop says: ". . . that whoever may have worn these ornaments, if they have served You faithfully, may merit to receive in heaven the crown which these signify." The virgin sings again:

I have despised the kingdom of the world and every worldly ornament, for the sake of the love of Our Lord Jesus Christ, whom I have seen, whom I have loved, in whom I have believed, of whom I have been very fond.

When about to place the wreath on the virgin's head, the Bishop invites her: "Come, spouse of Christ, receive the crown which the Lord has prepared for you in heaven." This he can say because the wreath he is placing on her head is a symbol of the wreath of glory she will receive as reward. Then he places the wreath on her head and prays:

Receive the crown of virginal excellence, that, just as you are crowned on earth by our hands, so you may merit to be crowned in heaven by Christ with glory and honor.

The lighted candle which is presented to the virgin is a symbol of virginal love, of total dedication to Christ as a sacrifice and a sacred trust.

The Eucharistic Sacrifice was celebrated after the virgin's consecration. This was really a wedding Banquet. By Holy Communion Christ as Spouse would enter the heart of the virgin and personally ratify the bond of eternal love with His bride. It seems that there was a time when because of special conditions the virgin was given enough Sacred Hosts to be able to give herself Holy Communion for eight days. This might be looked upon as a complete surrender of Christ into the hands of His chosen bride, to let her enjoy the mystic delights of His love during those days of His personal Presence.

Rightly, then, anyone who dedicates his lifetime to Christ by perfect and virginal chastity, may rejoice in having

Christ as mystic Spouse and enjoy His tender and intimate love.

A Prayer for the Choice of This Vocation

O my God and dearest Savior, I have been thinking of living in perfect chastity all my life, and to serve Your Church and my fellow men in the single state of the laity. If it is really Your will that I choose this splendid vocation, please grant me the grace to know Your will and to accept it gladly and courageously. Help me to come to a decision. In the meantime aid me with Your all-powerful graces to prepare well for this Christian ideal of living. Especially protect my purity against the attacks of the world and the Devil and against my own weaknesses. Through frequent participation in the Eucharistic Sacrifice and Sacrament let me grow daily in love for You by a spirit of prayer and of sacrifice for fellow men. Amen.

CHAPTER FIVE

The Manner of Dedication

WE HAVE EXPLAINED THAT PERFECT CHASTITY, TO HAVE ANY value for the spiritual nuptials with Christ, must be willed freely; or, in other words, one must dedicate himself to it. We shall now explain the various degrees in which that can be done.

First, one can make a simple resolution or promise to observe perfect chastity for a lifetime in the single state in the world, primarily, for the love of Christ, but secondarily for a more perfect devotion to social blessings of Church and mankind. In his letter *On Holy Virginity* (p. 163) the Holy Father acknowledges this form, a simple promise, for such a dedication. One may make such a promise without binding oneself to its observance under pain of sin. If one did get married after such a promise, there would be no sin, or if one did commit a sin against chastity, this would be a sin only against chastity but not against religion.

Secondly, one can make the dedication of one's life in perfect chastity by private vow, that is, by a promise to observe perfect chastity under the virtue of religion. In that case, if one would break the vow by committing sins against chastity, one would commit a twofold sin: one against chastity and one against religion. The very act of contracting marriage would be a sin, not against chastity, but against religion. In fact, by Church law the simple vow of virginity or of perfect chastity or of not getting married, makes the act of getting married without dispensation illicit, though not invalid (Canon Law, n. 1058, 1).* One would first have to get a dispensation from such a vow before getting married. Priests often have faculties through their Bishops for dispensing from such a perpetual vow that was made prior to the eighteenth year of age, as well as from a temporary vow (Cf. Canon Law, nn. 1313 and 1309). For dispensing from the vow of perfect and perpetual chastity made unconditionally and after the eighteenth year of age recourse must be had to the Holy See (Canon Law, n. 1309).

In any case, such a vow of perfect chastity by a lay person will be a private vow. It could be a public vow only if it were made in the name of the Church and accepted as such by a legitimate ecclesiastical superior. To make such a public vow was forbidden by the Holy See in 1927.[19] It is, however, not impossible that the Church might grant such a privilege in the future, as she had in the earlier centuries of the Church.**

The simple promise or private vow may be made merely with an internal resolution and no further formality. One could also recite a special prayer of consecration, privately, either in one's home or before an altar in Church. At the end of this chapter you will find an example of such a prayer of consecration.

We spoke of the twofold sin resulting from the violation of chastity if one has bound himself to it by vow. But it should be of greater interest that there is a twofold merit for the observance of chastity under vow: the merit of chastity itself and the merit of religion. By such a practice

---

*The author is referencing the 1917 Code of Canon Law, which was in effect until the new Code was promulgated in 1983. —*Publisher*, 2005.
**See Canon 604, "Order of Virgins." (1983 Code). —*Publisher*, 2005.

of the virtue of religion one does great honor to God and merits rich graces and beautiful glory. Besides, such a vow to live chastely brings stability into one's life and adds strength, psychologically, to the practice of the virtue. Pope Pius XII commends those who in the past have taken such a vow (*On Holy Virginity*, pp. 163, 166).

It would not be wise to bind oneself by a perpetual vow immediately. One should take the matter by steps. Ordinarily one should first make a promise that does not bind under sin, for example, for one year. If one passes this test and wishes to continue in that life of chastity, one may make a temporary vow binding oneself for one or three years; or one might make a temporary vow annually for three years. After that period of probation is over, one can and should make a perpetual vow. About the value of such a vow the Holy Father has this to say:

The Princes of Sacred Theology, too, St. Thomas Aquinas and St. Bonaventure, resting on the authority of St. Augustine,[20] teach that virginity does not possess the stability of virtue unless it springs from a vow made to keep virginity perpetually unsullied. Certainly, those who bind themselves by a perpetual vow to preserve virginity put into practice Christ's statement about perpetual abstinence from matrimony in the highest degree and most perfect manner. Nor can one justly assert that the resolve of those who wish to leave open for themselves some avenue of retreat from this resolve is better and more perfect. (*On Holy Virginity*, p. 165)

The form of life resulting from a firm will to live in perfect chastity permanently is a state of life, just as matrimony is; in other words, a real vocation. We said it is a "state of life"; we did not say that it is a "state of perfection." As is known, in the Church there are two states of perfection, recognized technically and officially as such: the priesthood and religious life. Virginal chastity in the world as a form of life is not such a technical and official state of perfection, though, of course, as we shall show later, it is a great boon for striving for perfection. It is, however, a state of life in the Church; that is, a permanent mode of living according to God's will, accepted as a distinct vocation from God, which sets it apart from the other vocations, namely, the priesthood, religious life, life in a secular institute, or married life. It is permanent by the will of the subject to live in perfect chastity for a lifetime. It is not merely a substitution for marriage or for the religious life. It is a true state of life independent of these, with its own proper mode of living and of striving for perfection. It is such a state of life even though sealed with only a promise. By comparison, there are congregations of religious that do not take vows but whose members are still considered being in a special state of life.

One might infer from the canon of the Council of Trent, preferring virginity to marriage, that the Church considers and always considered virginity a state of life on a par with, even superior to, that of matrimony. That was more evident in ancient times when virgins were granted civil and Church protection, and when they were publicly acknowledged as virgins, even consecrated officially as such. Pope Pius XII speaks of "the state of life" of the four daughters of the deacon Philip in Acts 21,9 (*On Holy Virginity*, p. 162).

Such members of the Mystical Body must, consequently, be cared for in a special way by priests, and must be respected by all, and not regarded as selfish bachelors and old maids. Often enough a girl while younger is esteemed highly in her community for her intelligence and competence. But as she grows older and her intention of remaining single becomes known, she is disregarded more and more. Such a condition should never exist in the Church of Christ.

True, because of the very mode of life chosen, single people might be isolated from the younger members of the parish who still have hopes of marriage as well as from the married groups. But, at least in larger cities, they could form a society of their own: the women perhaps under the patronage of the Blessed Virgin; the men under that of St. Joseph. Such men and women should never form one society of single people. That however does not exclude both from joining the same Third Order Fraternity, because here there is no distinction between married and unmarried; all strive for personal perfection.

That the single people should band together and organize somewhat seems natural. Today they are more or less a dispersed flock, socially and spiritually strangers to one another. They are also an isolated group, separated from all other groups in the parish. At times they are forsaken and without the proper spiritual care. Unconsciously they may tend to become individualistic, old-fashioned, and isolated from society at large.

Actually in the world of spirit they do form a kind of society, inasmuch as they all have Christ as Spouse, and all have the same spiritual ideals. In Scripture they are presented as forming a distinct, an élite, group (Apocalypse 14,1-5; Matthew 25,1-13).

The spirit of brotherly and sisterly love should animate them to band together for mutual encouragement and help. They are expected to labor in the apostolate of charity; certainly, they should care for each other first, women for women, and men for men. In such a society they could meet regularly, for instance, once a month, for "community" prayer and other spiritual exercises.

By banding together in a society after the example of the Holy Name Society or the Sodality of the Blessed Mother, they could form a distinct circle in the parish but at the same time fit harmoniously into the entire community.

Such a society could make legal protection for the members much easier, a thing that would certainly be beneficial, especially for the women. It would probably facilitate getting jobs for the members, especially for the women.

For the rest, whether they should also have a common house—never, of course, with men and women living under the same roof—might be disputed, since that would make them too much like a religious community. Soon some kind of superior would be needed, or at least an administrator, and a more or less complicated system of administration would be necessary. That would almost inevitably lead to forming a kind of religious society. In Europe there are some who advocate common houses for such single people. We shall touch upon the matter again under careers and a mode of livelihood.

Formula of Consecration

Most Sacred Heart of Jesus, I now dedicate (by a vow) my whole person, body and soul, to You as my Divine Spouse, to live in perfect chastity for . . . year(s) (my whole life), that I may please You more perfectly by a holy life, that I may enjoy more intimate and intense happiness with You in the glorious life of heaven, and that I may be able to help a greater number of fellow men to procure for themselves a peaceful life on earth and everlasting happiness in heaven. Amen.

CHAPTER SIX

Perfect Chastity a Boon for Church and Society

ONE CAN, AND REALLY SHOULD, CHOOSE THE SINGLE LIFE OF perfect chastity in the world for the secondary purpose of doing good for the Church and for society, both civic and cultural. Closely connected with this purpose of doing social good is the matter of earning a livelihood, commonly referred to as following a career. The idea of a career is interrelated with that of the apostolate, but we shall treat them in separate chapters.

Virgin souls are a great boon to Church and society. Pope Pius XII has this to say:

> We think it timely, moreover, briefly to touch upon the error of those who wish to turn youths away from seminaries, and girls from convents, and for that purpose try to impress upon their minds that today the Church has greater need of the help and practice of Christian virtues of those who are married and live a life in common with others in the world, than of priests and consecrated virgins, who because of the vow of chastity they have taken are almost withdrawn from human society. But there is no one, Venerable Brothers, who does not see that this opinion is utterly false and most disastrous. (*On Holy Virginity*, p. 177)

Those words of the Pope can be applied equally to attempts to dissuade young people from choosing the vocation of single chastity in the world. These are not lost to society. They are a great boon to society, because they are expected to take an even greater interest in the needs and benefits of society.

They must try to influence society by their *good example.* Even consecrated virgins in convents must work for the good of society, at least inasmuch as their good example will be of benefit to others. In the Prayer after the Mass for the Consecration of Virgins, the Bishop prays that the virgins may give others the example of good living. Much more, then, will people in the world be expected to set a good example to fellow men, and thus make the world a better place to live in. Very encouraging are these words of the Holy Father:

Finally, virginity that is consecrated to Christ is in itself such a witness to faith in regard to the Kingdom of heaven, and demonstrates such a love toward the Divine Redeemer, that there is little wonder that it produces abundant fruits of holiness. Indeed, the virgins and all those who dedicate themselves to the apostolate and consecrate themselves to perfect chastity, and who adorn the Church with the lofty holiness of their lives are almost innumerable. (*On Holy Virginity,* p. 172)

Such holiness of life is a splendid ideal set before all men of good will.

There is, moreover, *the apostolate of prayer.* Those who dedicate themselves to perfect chastity can exert a powerful influence on society through prayer in favor of their fellow men. They are most intimate friends, brides in fact, of the Creator Himself, from whom come all blessings. Their prayers must have a special efficacy. The Holy Father speaks of this apostolate too:

Besides, virginity is fruitful not merely because of the external enterprises and activities, to which those who embrace it can more easily and fully devote themselves, but also because of the forms of perfect charity toward fellow men, that is, because of the earnest prayers said for their benefit, and because of the severe trials gladly and freely endured for that same cause. To these forms the servants of God and the brides of Jesus Christ, especially those who spend their lives within convent walls, have consecrated their whole lives. (*On Holy Virginity*, p. 172)

Later he speaks of contemplatives thus:

Those, too, who live the contemplative life, precisely because they do not only offer their prayers and supplications to God, but because they offer to God also the immolation of themselves for the salvation of others, certainly contribute much to the good of the Church. (*On Holy Virginity*, p. 178)

What the Pope says directly of contemplatives in convents can readily be applied to people in the world who devote themselves to perfect chastity and take greater interest in prayer. It was in keeping with these ideas that St. Ambrose wrote:

You, parents, have heard in what virtues and lessons you ought to train your daughters, that by their merits your sins may be redeemed. The virgin is God's gift, the parents' offering, the priesthood of chastity. The virgin is an offering for her mother, by whose daily sacrifice the divine power is appeased. The virgin is the inseparable pledge of her parents, who does not seek a dowry, nor forsake them by leaving home, nor offend them by injuries. (*On Virgins*, Ch. 7, n. 32)[21]

People who live a single life in the world should, however, not regard spiritual exercises as the only way for exercising charity and being fruitful. They should be anxious to engage in *social charity* according to their ability and interests. The fields of work are many and vast. In his discourse of October 1945, Pope Pius XII stressed the usefulness of the unmarried for the Church, and for civic and political life. Again, in his discourse to the Cardinals on the occasion of the definition of the Assumption, November 2, 1950, he said:

> Where, however, marriages adorned with Christian virtues flourish intact, chaste virginity, nourished by love of Christ, flourishes with equal pace and progress. We ask you [the Cardinals] to exhort your clergy that they esteem highly the form of this noble life, which makes men like angels, that they foster it conscientiously and persuade others too to walk so noble a road of virtue, especially the women, because, if their concerted effort in the exercise of the apostolate languishes, the Church suffers much damage.[22]

Single people in the world, not being tied down by a marriage partner and family cares, are quite free to expend more time and energy on social works of all kinds. Apropos is what the Pope says in his encyclical about virginity being a liberation:

> Here We think it opportune, Venerable Brothers, to give a fuller and more careful explanation why the love of Christ spurs generous souls on to abstain from marriage, and what mystic relations exist between virginity and the perfection of Christian charity. Already in Jesus Christ's statement, which we quoted above, it is suggested that such perfect abstinence from marriage frees men from its grave offices and duties. . . . It is easy, therefore, to understand why those who desire to dedicate themselves to the divine service, embrace the state of virginal life as a kind of liberation, for the purpose, namely, of being able to serve God more fully and to contribute to the good of fellow men with all their power. (*On Holy Virginity*, p. 168)

He cites examples of Saints like Francis Xavier, Vincent de Paul, John Bosco, Mother Cabrini, and all they accomplished because they were unhindered by looking after the corporal and spiritual needs of wife or husband or children. Because the single have no dependents, they are able and willing to take difficult assignments, assignments in dangerous and trying posts of society. They are ready for unpleasant jobs; such jobs often fall to their lot "naturally."

Single people in the world are, in a sense, especially for certain types of charitable works, freer than priests and religious. They do not have to wait for the counsel or command of superiors before taking care of urgent works of mercy. More, they are lay people and have access where priests and religious might be unwanted.

People, therefore, often choose the single life in the world precisely because of all the opportunities it will afford them for doing social work, spiritual and corporal works of mercy. In this activity they really imitate their virgin Mother and Christ's Spouse, the Church, in her fruitfulness for souls. Just as the Church, so they devote themselves wholeheartedly to serving fellow men. Christ is the Spouse of the virgin heart, which He fills with His love, a love universal and sympathetic toward all members of the human family. Such love does not remain sterile. Rather it blossoms and is rich in fruitfulness. In a later chapter we shall show how the Fathers delighted in pointing out the relation between the virgin fruitfulness of our Mother Church and of the virgin souls. Bachelors and virgins for Christ's sake are, then, not wholly isolated from society, much less enemies of society. Though they forego a family of their own, they are a great blessing to the families of others by their social activity in favor of the family.

In virtue of this fruitfulness of virgin souls, women, though virgins, will be mothers in a metaphoric and mystic sense, but in a true sense. By this spiritual and supernatural motherhood they will bring forth many souls for heaven. They will help others to achieve their ultimate end, which must be also the ultimate end of physical motherhood: life everlasting in heaven. St. Augustine illustrates this very nicely. Suppose, he says, that some rich woman would spend much money to buy a large number of slaves, in order to make them Christians. She would thus give birth to members of Christ in greater number than any mother by physical birth; really, physical birth does not make children Christians, but baptism does. Then he completes his comparison by saying that the fruitfulness of virginity is greater than the fruitfulness of such a rich woman.[23]

Men, too, who live a single life for the sake of Christ's love will not be unproductive. With St. Paul they can say that they "are in labor again, until Christ is formed" in others (Galatians 4,19). As brides of Christ they, too, play the role of a woman in this spiritual regeneration. They could, on the other hand, be considered as being on the side of Christ the Bridegroom, and, together with the Church, they beget children for everlasting happiness with their heavenly Father, which is the ultimate end of earthly fatherhood. The Holy Father applies to all who toil in the apostolate what he had written in his Apostolic Exhortation, *Menti nostrae,* for the clergy:

By the law of celibacy the priest not only does not lose the office of fatherhood, but rather increases it immensely, since he begets offspring not for this earthly and transitory life, but for the heavenly and unending life. (*On Holy Virginity,* p. 172)[24]

Particularly are the single dedicated to the afflicted of mankind. What the Pope says directly about Sisters holds equally of single lay men and women.

And besides, We believe it is necessary to warn that it is entirely erroneous to assert that those who have dedicated themselves to perfect chastity are separated from the society of men, almost as foreigners. Consecrated virgins, who devote their lives to the service of the poor and the sick, without distinction of race, social rank, or religion, are they not intimately united with their miseries and their pains, are they not drawn to them with most tender affection, as if they were their mothers? (*On Holy Virginity*, p. 178)

Virgin souls have given their hearts to Christ and can be very sympathetic toward the afflictions of others. They can be very unselfish and are very near to the poor, the sick, the children, the aged. This generous sympathy is really their greatest protection against ridicule for living a virginal life. That is the tangible fruit of their lives which even the worldly are able to appreciate. Besides, their sacrifice of perfect chastity wins from Christ many a choice grace for others. How much good virgin souls have accomplished in the history of the Church cannot be calculated by the mathematics of this world.

By virtue of the sacraments of Baptism and Confirmation Catholics become partakers of the priesthood of Jesus Christ, not in the strict sense of the sacrament of Holy Orders, but in the broader sense that the Catholic Church is a "holy nation and a kingly priesthood" according to St. Peter's first epistle (2,5). All Catholics must, therefore, take a positive interest in promoting the welfare of others and of the entire Church. Virgin souls place themselves in a most favorable position for fulfilling this their obligation in an excellent way and for cooperating in making the Church more and more "a holy nation and a kingly priesthood."

In general, women should engage especially in work that answers to their motherly instinct. There are jobs of social good for which women are better fitted by nature, for instance, wherever a sympathetic understanding is needed. Women should prefer such jobs, all else being equal. Men will preferably take care of social work for which a fatherly attitude and a creative mind is needed.

Today women are not so limited as formerly in the fields of social work. They can engage in the education of all classes of people at all levels. Particularly in line with their vocation is the education of youth in Christian Doctrine, to which many are presently devoting themselves. Some of them are going in pairs to foreign missions in order to bring Christ's consoling and necessary message to others. Today there is an excellent opportunity for lay people, especially women, to join the faculties of parochial schools. There is very much work to be done through the St. Vincent de Paul Society and the Legion of Mary.

There is also ample opportunity for helping around the parish church and rectory, for instance, in repairing and making altar linens and vestments, in doing secretarial work or house work. For all such work they certainly may, and ordinarily should, get a living wage. They should always get sufficient time for spiritual exercises, including daily Mass and Communion if they desire this. It does not make sense that people who devote themselves unstintingly to the temporal care of priests should deprive themselves of the spiritual services that every parishioner is entitled to, and that many actually enjoy.

For the rest, any work that is not directly concerned with the apostolate of souls comes more directly under the notion of careers, about which we shall speak next.

CHAPTER SEVEN

Careers and Home Life

PEOPLE WHO CHOOSE THE VOCATION OF THE SINGLE LIFE in the world must provide for themselves the temporal needs of food, clothing, and shelter. This they must do not merely for the present, but also for the future, when on account of sickness or old age they can no longer work. This need of providing for themselves holds especially for women. When a woman marries, she can normally expect her husband to provide for the home while she takes care of it. If she remains single, she must provide for herself. Of course, if she stays in the parental home to care for aged parents or orphaned brothers and sisters, she will have a home at least for awhile.

It is not possible in a book of this nature to name or describe all the careers and jobs that are open today, particularly for women who remain single. We shall rather give some principles according to which people who intend to live a virginal life in the world may choose their life's work, their avocation. For more detailed information on the individual jobs and professions books by specialists in the field may be consulted.

First, because of the needs described, the single person

must choose a career that will secure for him or her sufficient income for a livelihood and be provision against
sickness or old age. Because of this the career should be
of such a nature, if possible, that it will afford a job for
many years, even when one is older. Old age pensions are
a big help, and one may make use of them; but one should
not count entirely on them and should rather "make hay
while the sun shines." That is not so difficult today, even
for women, because there are many opportunities outside
the home, in the various professions and arts and sciences,
in industry and social works. We might recall here that
Pope Pius XII encouraged the women to insist on a just
wage, equal to a man's on the same level and output.[24a]

Second, one should choose a career for which he has the
necessary talent and education, or for which he is able to
acquire the education. One would invite failure were he
to choose a career for which he did not have the talents, for
instance, as a social worker or a teacher. Here, too, there
is a better chance for women today, because of the opportunities of higher education.

Third, one should choose a career that will not only not
endanger his ideal of virginal chastity, but in which he
can cherish that ideal constantly. This will often mean
choosing a career according to the next principle.

Fourth, some may wish to choose a career with a view to
working for the Church as much as possible. They will,
therefore, choose some phase of Catholic Action. To do
so is certainly in keeping with the entire ideal of a virginal
life in the world, dedicated to Christ and His cause. Such
would be full-time work for the Legion of Mary.

Fifth, others may desire a career with a view to bettering
society. Such would be the career of a lawyer or teacher in
a secular college, of a doctor or a nurse, of a writer or a
lecturer. The pay may not be so good as in some other

position, but one would have a greater and more lasting influence for good. This "Christopher" principle is an excellent one for those who devote their lives to serving Christ and His interests.

Sixth, we must single out political careers, because in them one can be most influential for the good of the nation and of Christ's Church, and because the Holy Father stressed this as a field of action open today in particular for women.[25]

Seventh, by mentioning the above careers specifically we do not wish to exclude any career in which a single person may honorably engage. For instance, any of the fine arts, painting, sculpturing, music, dramatics with its vast possibilities on radio and television, all present wonderful opportunities for Christian inspiration and social good. On the other hand, careers that call for manual labor are by no means excluded. Manual labor belongs to dignified work as well as other types of work.

Whatever the career, single people in love with Christ can be the greatest blessing to Church, to family, to society at large, whether in its civic or its cultural life.

A few ideas on how to work might prove beneficial. First, love the work of your apostolate and career. Do not endure it merely as a necessary evil. Follow the maxim: "What you do, do well." Second, work with a spirit of progress and improvement, with a spirit of wanting to better your job or profession wherever and whenever possible. Third, work perseveringly and patiently, undaunted by trials and difficulties. Fourth, do not work feverishly, so that you are practically always fatigued physically and worn out nervously. Occasionally, of course, one may be called on to do an extra amount of work, for which true heroism is required. Heroism however should ordinarily not have to be exercised by over-work. Especially, allow yourself enough time and energy for spiritual exercises, for the regular reception of the Sacraments, assistance at Mass, and a daily program of prayer. Fifth, take the needed and well-deserved rest and recreation each day, and also the periodical vacations. This will make working at your career more pleasant and interesting and efficient. Sixth, work unselfishly in the apostolate and humbly, in a spirit of cooperation for the best interests of Christ's Church, not your own ostentation. Seventh, where moral principles are involved, always be truly Catholic; follow the teaching of the Popes on labor. Eighth, join a union. That is worthwhile for single women for legal protection.

When people get married, they agree to establish a home of their own, even though they do not always have a house immediately. When one becomes a religious or a priest, one gets a dwelling. When a person decides to live a single life of perfect chastity in the world, he must often provide some kind of dwelling for himself.

For a man this is not too difficult. But he too, if at all possible, should have some place that he can call his own home, where he can hang his hat undisturbed and enjoy the quiet of solitude.

For a woman this problem is more acute. She is not able to live just anywhere, as a man may, especially if she is poor. It is also more difficult for a woman to live in certain dwellings than in others without endangering her vocation. But even for her there are various possibilities with varying desirability. Home is so much a part of a woman's happiness that the single woman too should choose her home wisely.

She might live with relatives: with parents as long as they are living, or with a brother or a sister. This would be an ideal arrangement, especially if she can have a room all to herself, and if she can live peaceably with the others. That would give her a home atmosphere and companion-ship, which she sacrificed in part by the vocation she chose. But she should know her place and not make attempts to steal the affections of the wife. Further, she should not be too attached to this home atmosphere; that is the test of her virginal love for Christ; it is the sacrifice she has made. What we have just said can, with proper adjustments, be applied to bachelors.

If one is well-to-do, one might have one's own home. It could perhaps be rented to a family, while retaining a suite of rooms for oneself. It would be good to do one's own cooking if at all possible; or at least some of the time. That is ordinarily better than always eating out. The drudgery of household work, even for the bachelor, is good discipline. It might be advisable to take in others of the same sex who have chosen the same form of life. Of course, then the problem of house rules and budgeting will have to be agreed on.

If a group of the same sex would be too poor to own their own house, they could perhaps pool their interests and rent an apartment. This has worked out in some cases. But the group should not be too large, or else problems of adminis-tration and of caring for the place arise. Recall the remarks we made above on this matter. Two or three should work out well.

On no condition should a man and a woman, or several of each sex, go partnership in housekeeping. That would soon be the death of perfect chastity. Besides, scandals would arise as they did in the earlier centuries of the Church.

In any case, prudence, charity, and a spirit of poverty and

self-denial will find a way to solve special problems. Of course, such chosen souls who have dedicated themselves to Christ in perfect chastity can bank very heavily on the all-good Providence of God.

Other matters about social life will be discussed in the last chapter.

Chapter Eight

The Excellence and Fruits of Perfect Chastity

THE FACT THAT THE PERFECTLY CHASTE SOUL IS A CONSE-
crated spouse of Christ brings out with crystal clarity the
excellence and the fruitfulness of this vocation in this life
and in the next.

Virginal love might be called the pearl of great price, of
which Christ speaks in His parable (cf. Matthew 13,14).
It is really one of the most priceless pearls in Christ's religion. Not without reason, then, is this parable used as
antiphon for the *Benedictus* in the Office of Virgins.
Virginal or perfect chastity is a very special gift of the
Redeemer to mankind. Pope Pius XII said it is "without
doubt among the most precious treasures which the Author
of the Church has left as heritage to the society which
He founded" (*On Holy Virginity*, p. 161), and is "a lofty
gift which was brought by the Christian religion" (p. 161).
It is the sweetest gift with which He endowed His own
Immaculate Mother, Mary, and His immaculate Spouse,
the Church. It is a supernatural gift of God, which makes
the virginal and chaste soul, just as the Church herself, a
bride coming down from heaven in all her beauty (cf.
Apocalypse 21,2), a vision of loveliness. It is because of

this that the virgin, at her consecration, after receiving the ring, sings the words that have been ascribed to St. Agnes:

I have been espoused to Him whom the angels serve, at whose beauty the sun and moon are in admiration. My Lord Jesus Christ has given me His ring as a pledge, and has adorned me with a wreath as His spouse.

An earthly bride shares in the dignity and inheritance of the bridegroom. Christ's bride shares in His dignity and in His treasures. By His grace He ennobles and beautifies His bride from within. He does not merely give her a dress, however rich and beautiful. He also raises her to His own status, as much as that is possible for a creature. If an earthly king gives royal rank to the peasant lady whom he marries, how much more will not the heavenly King give His regal honor and glory to His bride of chaste love. In a sense, then, this excellence of being Christ's bride is in itself the greatest reward that virginal and chaste love knows.

Virginal and chaste love consecrated to Christ makes the person a special bride of Christ, very much like Christ Himself. St. Bonaventure tells us that virginity is most praiseworthy by reason of the superadded beauty that comes from the special conformity to Christ the Spouse, to whom virginity conforms virgins in regard to excellence of virtue, of beauty, and of dignity (*On Evangelical Perfection*, q. 3, a. 3).[26] It is, in fact, the deep desire to be like to Christ even in virginal chastity that motivates many a soul to live such a life. Christ was the most pure Virgin, born of a most pure Virgin Mother. His dearest friends, too, were His Virgin Mother, His virgin father, St. Joseph, and John, the virgin disciple, most beloved of Jesus. In a sense, then, virginity and perfect chastity allow the soul to enjoy the delightful company of the most holy Virgin Mary, as is expressed in the Consecration of Virgins, after the giving of the ring. It also introduces one into the delightful company of St. Joseph and of all other virginal saints.

This sharing in the dignity of the Divine Bridegroom means changing one's former state of life and living an altogether new mode of life, far superior to the former. Pope Pius XII, in his homily for the canonization of Marianna Paredes of Jesus, dared to quote Didymus Alexander to the effect that virginity is "something divine." [27]

To live in virginity or perfect chastity is by no means a loveless life, as some adversaries would make believe. Love, in fact, is the very heart of virginity and perfect chastity— love of Christ and love of fellow men. But this love is not one-sided, as if we loved Christ and fellow men but received no love in return. Not at all. Christ loved us first as John and Paul would say. And really, a very intrinsic effect of espousal with Christ is to be loved by Him in a very intimate manner. This love is not merely well-wishing on Christ's part. His love is effective as well as affective. His love lavishes choicest gifts on His bride. The graces He gives His chaste bride are of the finest. Christ's love for His bride is invincible. If ever Paul's words were true, they are true of virginal and chaste lovers of Christ:

Who shall separate us from the love of Christ? Shall tribulation, or distress, or persecution, or hunger, or nakedness, or danger, or the sword? Even as it is written, "For your sake we are put to death all the day long. We are regarded as sheep for the slaughter."

But in all these things we overcome because of him who has loved us. For I am sure that neither death, nor life, nor angels, nor Principalities, nor things present, nor things to come, nor powers, nor height, nor depth, nor any other creature will be able to separate us from the love of God, which is in Christ Jesus our Lord. (Romans 8,35-39)

The virginal and chaste souls are the élite of Christ, privileged to follow Him in heaven wherever He goes (Apocalypse 14,4). We can suppose, then, that already in this world they are privileged people, who live in Christ's closest company, because they have made themselves so much like Him. They are the elect entourage of Christ the King (cf. Psalm 44,12).

The heavenly Spouse cares with special solicitude for those who follow Him in virginal and perfect chastity. He protects them, consoles them, helps them, rejoices their hearts. Just as of old, God cared for His bride, the true Israel: He fed her with the manna and gave her the drink of miraculous water; just as Christ cared for, cleansed and sanctified His bride, the Church, in the blood of His cross (cf. Ephesians 5, 22-32); just as He protects and strengthens her in time of persecution: just so does He sanctify, protect and strengthen His virginal and chaste brides. Of this protection and strength there are many miraculous witnesses in the history of the Saints, for example, St. Agnes, St. Lucy, St. Agatha, St. Mary Goretti.

That Christ might care for and protect His virginal brides is the repeated prayer of the Church in the Consecration of Virgins. For instance, at the imposition of the veil: "May He defend you against all evil and lead you to life eternal." At the blessing of the rings: "having been fortified by heavenly virtue." At the giving of the ring the Bishop says: "I espouse you to Jesus Christ . . . May He guard you unharmed." But the most beautiful prayer is in the Preface:

O Lord, through the gift of Your Spirit, may there be in them prudent modesty, wise kindness, serious gentleness, chaste freedom. May they be fervent in charity, and may they love nothing apart from You. May they live in a praiseworthy manner, but may they not seek to be praised. May they glorify You in holiness of body, and in the purity of their souls. May they fear You in love, may they serve You in love. May You be their honor, their joy, their desire; may You be their solace in sadness, their counsel in doubt, their defense in injury, their patience in tribulation, their abundance in poverty, their food in fasting, their medicine in sickness. In You may they have all things—in You whom they seek above all things to love. Through You may they safeguard what they have professed.

Though the virginal and chaste brides of Christ are always in the company of the Divine Spouse, He pays them very special visits from time to time. He has many surprise gifts of graces for them, after the manner of the surprise joy for Mary Magdalene when she was looking for Him in the garden of the resurrection. His visits may at times be in the form of trials, because the virginal life is not a trial-less mode of living. In fact, because He loves His bride, He will often try her with special sufferings. Of chaste souls especially is true what the Word says to the Beloved Disciple: "As for me, those whom I love I rebuke and chastise" (Apocalypse 3,19).

Being in the company of Jesus as Spouse will mean living with Him in closest spiritual intimacy, enjoying the sweet delight and peaceful joy of converse with Him in prayer. In such bridal converse Jesus shares His heavenly secrets with her. If, as He said, He makes all things known to His friends (John 15,14), He will surely be most generous in sharing His knowledge with His spouses. If, as He said, the Father reveals Himself to the little ones (cf. Matthew 11,25), He will certainly reveal Himself and His Son to the brides of this His Son.

This explains why the chaste brides of Our Lord have been admitted to such high degrees of contemplation and wisdom. They live under a heavenly fluorescent light of peculiar brightness and mellowness. Think of St. Gertrude and St. Margaret Mary and St. Gemma Galgani and St. Thérèse. Christ loves to reveal Himself to the pure who devote themselves more wholeheartedly to prayer. That is as it should be, since, according to St. Thomas, the end of a virginal life is contemplation (*Summa Theologica*, Part 2, of the 2d part, q. 132, a. 2 and 4). That truth was contained already in St. Paul's doctrine that a virgin can devote herself more completely to God and to prayer (1 Corinthians 7,8.40). St. Bonaventure, too, assures us that virginity disposes the soul more for contemplation, for which the greatest purity is necessary (*On Evangelical Perfection*, q. 3, a. 3).[28]

At no time, it seems, is Jesus so lavish with His love and intimate delights for His virgin brides as at Holy Communion. That, too, is as it should be. Then He is nearest, in this world, to the bride. As the Communion anthem for the Consecration of Virgins sings: "I have received honey and milk from His mouth, and His blood adorns my cheeks."

Spouses live for each other in a very special way. Christ, too, lives for the virgin bride, and she lives for Him. In the words of the bride of the Canticle: "My lover belongs to me and I to him; he browses among the lilies" (Canticle 6:3). St. Paul's gem in Galatians 2,20 is most true of Christ's chaste bride: "It is no longer I that live, but Christ lives in me." The chaste soul is in a more perfect sense the dwelling of God (2 Corinthians 6,16), as even the Preface of the Consecration of Virgins sings: "God, who has established Your dwelling in the pure heart," and again, "God, the benign Guest of chaste bodies." The heart of Christ's virgin bride is pre-eminently His very throne, from it He rules over her, and she reigns with Him. The chorus, therefore, chants: "Come, my beloved, and I shall set up my throne in you, because the King has desired your beauty."

Pope Pius XII, in his letter on virginity insists that, though virginity is more perfect than marriage, it is not necessary for Christian perfection (p. 178). Then he explains:

Sanctity of life can really be achieved even without chastity that is dedicated to God. For that we have the frequent witness of the sainted men and women who are honored by the Church with public cult, who were faithful spouses and splendid examples of excellent fathers and mothers of families. Indeed, it is not rare that one finds married people who are very earnest in striving for Christian perfection. (*On Holy Virginity*, p. 179)

In other words, virginal chastity, as such, is not the end of Christian perfection. That end is charity. And yet, precisely because of its relation to charity, is perfect chastity such a powerful means to perfection. Virginal love, by its very purpose, makes possible the perfection of charity, that virtue of perfection, that queen of all virtues. In its positive aspect, virginal or perfect chastity is an undivided and everlasting love of Christ and God. That is perfect love. It also frees a person for a wholehearted service of fellow men, as we explained earlier. It makes possible a more perfect practice of charity in general and in particular through Catholic Action. What the Pope wrote is apropos:

If, therefore, virginity, as we have written, is more excellent than matrimony, that comes undoubtedly chiefly from the fact that it aspires to achieve a more excellent end; and that, moreover, it also has the greatest efficacy for dedicating oneself entirely to the divine service, while, on the other hand, the heart of one who is tied down by the bonds and business of marriage is more or less "divided" (1 Corinthians 7,33). (*On Holy Virginity*, p. 179)

Little wonder, then, that, in the words of the Pope,

The virgins and all those who dedicate themselves to the apostolate and consecrate themselves to perfect chastity, and who adorn the Church with the lofty holiness of their lives are almost innumerable. (*On Holy Virginity*, p. 172)

It is worth while, too, to recall what the Pope said about "the mystic relations [that] exist between virginity and the perfection of Christian charity" (p. 168), which we quoted earlier. We must call attention here to our earlier treatment of the fruitfulness of the virgin souls for the good of Church and society.

In its negative aspect virginal and perfect chastity is an unequalled means to holiness. It is in itself a courageous form of self-denial. It demands complete dominion over the passions. The chaste person is ruled by the spirit, not by the flesh. Chastity subdues one of the greatest hindrances to perfection—the rebellion of the flesh, which distracts our attention from God and from heavenly interests. Again the words of the Holy Father are to the point:

There is, further, another reason why all those who sincerely desire to consecrate themselves to God and the salvation of fellow men, embrace the state of virginity. The holy Fathers certainly expressed that reason when discussing the advantages that those can have who abstain entirely from such corporal pleasures precisely that they may take greater delight in the exaltation of the spiritual life. As the holy Fathers themselves noted, pleasure of this kind, which is lawful when it arises from marriage, is not to be reproved in itself; why, chaste marriage is ennobled and sanctified by a special sacrament. Nevertheless, it must likewise be admitted that the lower faculties of human nature, after the wretched fall of Adam, are opposed to right reason and at times even impel man to do what is dishonorable. (*On Holy Virginity*, p. 169)

From this aspect, as well as from the fact that through perfect chastity one foregoes an otherwise lawful pleasure in married life and offers it to God—from this aspect perfect chastity is a real sacrifice. By it the brides of Christ "present" their "bodies as a sacrifice, living, holy, pleasing to God"—their "spiritual service" (Romans 12,1). Quoting St. Ambrose, in view of the vigilance and struggle needed to preserve virginity, Pope Pius XII writes: "For virginity, according to Ambrose,[29] is a kind of sacrifice, and the virgin herself is an oblation of modesty, a victim of chastity" (*On Holy Virginity*, p. 180). With that in mind, St. Ambrose spoke of the soul of a virgin as the altar "on which Christ is daily immolated for the redemption of the body." [30] Already St. Methodius had written at length on the idea that virginity is a sacrifice and that the virgin is herself the altar on which the sacrifice is offered, a sacrifice that is the more perfect the more completely one observes modesty as well as chastity.[31] For instance, he has the Virgin Thallousa say:

For I am persuaded, having learned this thoroughly from the Sacred Writings, that the greatest and most glorious offering and gift, to which nothing that men can offer to God is comparable, is the struggle for virginity.[32]

From both the positive and negative aspect, it follows that perfect and virginal chastity is a form of martyrdom, a daily dying to self. Since this is endured for the love of Christ, the Fathers have rightly thought of virginity as the culmination of perfect charity toward Christ. That is why so many who were willing and able to keep their virginity intact were also ready and generous in preserving it by the supreme sacrifice of martyrdom. How many virgins have not sealed their resolution of perfect chastity with their own blood! How often does not hagiography note that such and such a Saint gained the twofold reward: the crown of chastity and the palm of martyrdom; or that perfect chastity was crowned by martyrdom! And why not? The Pope explains:

Really, virginity inspires souls with such spiritual strength that, if necessary, it can urge one on even to martyrdom. History teaches that very clearly by proposing a host of so many virgins for the admiration of all, from St. Agnes of Rome to St. Mary Goretti. (*On Holy Virginity*, p. 172)

The Holy Father notes, too, that St. Methodius compared virgins to martyrs,[33] and that St. Gregory the Great taught that perfect chastity substitutes for martyrdom:[34]

For, though there is no occasion for persecution, still our peace has its martyrdom, because, even though we do not place our necks of flesh under the sword, still in our minds we slay the carnal desires with the spiritual sword. (*On Holy Virginity*, p. 180)

Later the same Pope praises those virgins and chaste souls, the world over, who today are bravely persevering in their vocation of perfect chastity, even though it often means death (*ibid.*, p. 190).

Virginity and perfect chastity not only make the perfection of charity easier, but they nourish all the other virtues. Pius XI summed that up thus:

When it is present, all virtues flourish; when absent, they are in danger. Purity feeds the light of the mind, the generosity of the heart, the strength of the soul, and even the health of the body. (*Discourse on the Centenary of St. Aloysius*, Dec. 30, 126)[35]

All this about the advantage of perfect chastity for holiness easily disposes of the objections that some Catholics have made in late years that marriage is better because it is a sacrament and virginity is not. We saw earlier how the Pope censured that opinion. He explained that, though the sacrament of matrimony strengthens the bonds of mutual affection between husband and wife, "nevertheless, it was not instituted in order to make the use of marriage a more suitable means in itself for uniting the souls of spouses with God Himself by the bonds of charity" (*On Holy Virginity*, p. 175). If that were true, why should the Apostle Paul have advised couples to abstain from the conjugal act for a time, in order that they might devote themselves more freely to prayer, asks the Pope (p. 176).

Nor is the "mutual help," which is sought in Christian marriage, and actually found there, a more effective means for striving for personal holiness than "the solitude of the heart" of virgins and celibates. The opposite error was refuted by the Pope, whose words are worth quoting in full:

For, although all those who embrace the state of perfect chastity have renounced such human love; nevertheless, on that account one may not affirm that because of this privation they have diminished and despoiled their human personality. Really, these receive from the Giver of heavenly gifts Himself something spiritual that indeed surpasses immensely "the mutual help" that spouses give to each other. Since they dedicate themselves entirely to Him who is their beginning and who shares with them His divine life, they do not diminish themselves, but increase themselves in the greatest degree possible. Who, indeed, can apply to themselves more truly than virgins this wonderful assertion of the Apostle Paul: "It is now no longer I that live, but Christ lives in me" (Galatians 2,20). (*On Holy Virginity*, p. 176 f.)

In heaven, according to Our Lord's own teaching, people neither marry nor are given in marriage. He explains: "For neither shall they be able to die any more, for they are equal to the angels, and are sons of God, being sons of the resurrection" (Luke 20,36). The resurrection is, therefore, the key to why men do not marry in heaven and live like angels. The glorified body is immortal and has the properties of a soul, of the angelic spirits. There is no need of marriage or reason for it among the glorified in heaven. Those who on earth forego marriage and live in virginal and chaste love begin here below to live like the angels, like pure spirits, unhindered by the craving of the flesh. It is the idea of St. Cyprian that they share already on earth in the resurrection, and for that reason live an angelic life. The Pope quotes from him:

Nor is virginity called the angelic virtue without reason. St. Cyprian rightly tells us that much when writing to virgins: "What we are to be you have already begun to be. You already possess the glory of the resurrection in this world; you pass through the world without being contaminated by the world. When you persevere in being chaste and virgins, you are like the angels of God." (*On the Apparel of Virgins*, Ch. 22).[36] (*On Holy Virginity*, p. 172 f.)

That is the reason for the age-old tradition—recorded by Tertullian at the beginning of the third century[37]—that virginal life is angelic. The ceremony of Consecration of Virgins in its Preface expresses it thus: "And, though still bound by the condition of mortal men, you already ascend to the likeness of the angels"; and it calls the virgin "the rival of angelic integrity." Pope Pius XII in his homily for the canonization of St. Mary Goretti said: "Virginity is a kind of angelic life,[38] which the Christian religion extols to such a high degree of beauty that it seems greater than earth and worthy of heaven." [39]

We have, then, in this the basic reason for speaking of virginal and chaste living as heavenly. The state of consecrated virginity and chastity permits one to realize already in this life what is essentially the supreme vocation and goal of every intelligent creature: union with Christ in heaven, in a purely spiritual life, without interest in the material needs of the body or the cravings of the passions.

When Christ counselled virginal chastity, He gave as the motive "for the kingdom of heaven's sake" (Matthew 19,12). That is the motive because it is the reward. The reward expected and to be received for living a life of perfect chastity is heaven itself. That is the greatest and most forceful motive for living such a life. Perfect chastity, in other words, merits and secures an eternal happiness not merely in the ordinary sense, but in a very special sense and degree.

That there will be a very special happiness for the virginal bride of Christ is revealed in the Apocalypse 14,4 (where the virgins are said to follow the Lamb wherever He goes), as well as in Christ's statement about choosing this form of life "for the kingdom of heaven's sake." And, even though "pure of heart" in Christ's Beatitudes does not refer specifically to inner chastity, it does include this in a very particular way. Christ's promise then: "Blessed are the pure of heart, for they shall see God" (Matthew 5,8), holds pre-eminently for virginal purity.

Perfect chastity merits in a particular fashion the vision of Christ and God; it merits a special intensity of loving Christ and of being loved by Him. In the Consecration of Virgins the virgin sings:

Behold, what I have longed for I already see; what I hoped for, I already possess: in heaven I am united with Him whom, while I was on earth, I loved with all my heart.

Perfect chastity merits a special fulness of joy for having renounced the carnal pleasures on earth and for having tried to find true happiness in spiritual things, in Christ especially. Perfect chastity, in short, merits a most intimate union with Christ and the Triune God in heaven.

Virginal chastity, for having willed to keep the body sacred and inviolate in this life, merits in an eminent degree incorruption of the body and a glorious splendor. We may note the consistency with which the Church has, through the centuries, argued from the perfect virginity of Mary to her incorruption and glorious Assumption, thus indicating the close relation that exists, according to God, between the incorruption of a virginal body and the incorruption of a glorified body.

Furthermore, in his Apocalypse (14,4) St. John reveals that virgins have the promise of the very special honor of following the Lamb in heaven wherever He goes, and of singing a song so sublime that only these virgins can join the chorus. That seems to be true also symbolically, inasmuch as the virgin souls will have an incomparable joy in being with Christ. This particular honor and privilege will be a special halo of glory that Christ will grant to His chaste brides. St. Augustine, commenting on that passage of Apocalypse, has a picturesque description of the joys of virgin souls in heaven:

Where do we think this Lamb goes where no one either dares or is able to follow save you? Where do we think He goes? Into what glades and meadows? I think, where the grass are joys, not the vain joys of this world, deceptive madnesses; nor joys such as shall be in the kingdom of God itself for the rest who are not virgins; but joys distinct from the lot of joys of all the rest. The joy of Christ's virgins is about Christ, in Christ, with Christ, after Christ, through Christ, on account of Christ. The joy of the virgins of Christ is not the same as of those who are not virgins, although these are of Christ. Really, for different persons there are different joys, but to none other are there such joys. Go and enter into these; follow the Lamb, because the flesh of the Lamb too is indeed virgin. (*On Holy Virginity,* Ch. 27, n. 27)[40]

In the Consecration of Virgins the idea of eternal reward for a life of perfect chastity is the constant refrain. At the blessing of the veil the Bishop prays: "May they merit to enter the nuptials of everlasting happiness." At the giving of the veil he says: "Receive the holy veil, the emblem of chastity and modesty; may you carry it before the judgment seat of Our Lord Jesus Christ, that you may have eternal life, and may live forever and ever." With the giving of the ring the Bishop prays: "Receive, then, the ring of faith, the seal of the Holy Spirit, that you may be called the Spouse of God, and, if you serve Him faithfully, may wear a crown forever." After the giving of the ring, he petitions "that you may merit to receive the crown of virginity." For the blessing of the wreath he says: "That whoever wears these [ornaments], if she has served You faithfully, may merit to receive in heaven the crown which these symbolize." When placing the wreath on the virgin's head, he says: ". . . so you may merit in heaven to be crowned by Christ with glory and honor." Later in the Secret of the

Mass he petitions: "That, at the coming of the Sovereign King, when the doors have opened wide, they [the virgins] may merit to enter the heavenly kingdom with joy." In the Preface the idea of eternal reward is expressed very nicely:

> May those who are about to enter a union, not of the body, but of the mind, with Him who scrutinizes the hearts, cross over to the number of wise maidens, that, with the oil of preparedness, they may await the heavenly Spouse with the lighted lamps of virtues. Nor should they be disturbed by a sudden coming of the King, but they should meet Him joyfully and confidently, guided by the light and accompanied by the choir of virgins who have gone before. And may they not be excluded with the foolish virgins, but may they, with the wise virgins, freely enter through the royal doorway, and remain in the company of Your Lamb forever. Through Your favor may they merit to be adorned with a hundredfold fruit, the gift of virginity.

That leads us to the last consideration of this reward, the joy. Since a wedding is considered one of the most joyful events experienced in this world, the figure of a wedding is used often to describe the joy of heaven. This figure is so much more apt for a virgin bride, because the possession of heaven by her is a spiritual wedding. That is why in the Consecration of Virgins the reward of a virgin is described in the language of Christ's parable of a marriage feast, which the prudent virgins are privileged to attend (Matthew 25,1-13), and in the language of the nuptials of the Church with Christ as revealed in the Apocalypse (19,7).

"Come" is a repeated invitation in the ceremony of the Consecration of Virgins. "Come" is the language of the Spouse for His bride to join Him in everlasting happiness. Virginity and perfect chastity have necessarily and essentially an eschatologic outlook: they look forward to the "last things," to a heavenly life through endless ages with the beloved Spouse. Bridal love, more than any other love, desires union of the lovers. That union will be most complete in heaven.

All this excellence and reward of virginal and perfect chastity adds up to one thing: a life of genuine peace and joy already in this world, and of hope for even better things in the next. This is the peace that only Christ can give (John 14,27), and which He truly gives, so much so that chaste and virginal espousal with Christ is a peace pact with Him. Christ could very well adapt God's promise to Israel of old: "I will make a covenant of peace with them; it shall be an everlasting covenant with them" (Ezechiel 37, 26).

Christ's bride can be joyful in Christ because of the anticipated joy of paradise. This is a joy that is delightful, above the sweetest love on earth. It must be tasted to be appreciated.

Because of the heavenly reward, the life of virginal love is most hopeful; but especially is the death of such a soul full of hope and delight. It is indeed sweet to die, when with the lamp of the prudent virgin one can meet the Lord and Judge as Spouse. When St. Thérèse knew that she would soon die, she exclaimed: "It is about time that we see each other." The very thought of death inspires joy not fear, because it will be the day of the wedding, when Christ will come to take home His virgin bride. It is the day when He will invite: "Come, Bride of Christ, receive the crown that the Lord has prepared for you forever." Nor will the thought of judgment be fearful, because the Judge is Himself the virgin's Spouse. Like the virginal Stephen, the virgin bride will at death see the heavens open and there behold Christ in all His glory (cf. Acts 8,56). At death the bride will hear the good news of Martha to Mary: "The Master is here and calls for you" (John 11,28).

The thought, then, of this great day should be always uppermost in the mind of Christ's brides and should be an inspiration for living as chastely as possible. The virgins should long for this great day. "Where your treasure is, there your heart also will be" (Matthew 6,20).

Several times in his letter *On Holy Virginity* the Holy Father speaks of virginity and perfect chastity as "the beautiful virtue" (pp. 182, 187). He is thereby voicing an age-old tradition, which expressed this idea in the words of the Latin Vulgate of Wisdom 4,1: "Oh how beautiful is the chaste generation with glory, for the memory thereof is immortal, being known both to God and to men." Practically all the Churchmen who wrote a treatise on virginity stressed, sometimes at great length, the beauty of virginity and the virginal nuptials, especially because of the incomparable beauty of the Divine Spouse. St. Ambrose is worth quoting:

And observe how great a kingdom the Holy Spirit has assigned to you by the testimony of the divine Scriptures—gold and beauty. . . . Gold, because as that metal is more precious when tried by fire, so the loveliness of the virginal body, consecrated to the Divine Spirit, increases its own comeliness. Who can imagine a comeliness greater than the beauty of her who is loved by the King, approved by the Judge, dedicated to the Lord, consecrated to God; ever a bride, ever unmarried, so that neither love has an end nor modesty any harm. (*On Virgins*, Bk. 1, Ch. 7, n. 37)[41]

And again,

First, inasmuch as those who are about to marry desire above all else, to boast of the beauty of their spouse, they must of necessity confess that they are inferior to consecrated virgins, who alone can say: "You are beautiful above the sons of men, grace is poured out on your lips" (Psalm 44,2). Who is this Spouse? One not given to vile services, not proud of perishable riches, but one whose throne is forever and ever. The King's daughters are in His honor: "The queen stood on your right hand, in gilded clothing; surrounded with variety" (Psalm 44, 10). (*On Virgins*, Bk. 1, Ch. 7, n. 36)[42]

In the language of the Canticle, the Divine Spouse can sing of every chaste soul espoused to Him: "You are beautiful as Thersa, my beloved, as lovely as Jerusalem" (Canticle 6,4), and, "You are beautiful, my beloved, and there is no blemish in you" (Canticle 4,7).

Our Holy Father quotes St. Thomas as saying that "to virginity is attributed the most excellent beauty," [43] and then remarks that "this undoubtedly explains why virgins captivate all by their example" (*On Holy Virginity*, p. 173). Virginal chastity is essentially interior; it is the integrity of the mind never to make use of the power of sex, without or within marriage. Hence a woman remains a virgin even if she has been deflowered against her will. And yet bodily virginal integrity is something to be prized, as is evidenced by the miraculous protection of it in the Blessed Virgin Mother of Christ. It does add a special luster and fresh fragrance to the inner beauty of chastity. But one must not make the mistake of equating virginal beauty with beauty of the body. Virginal chastity is essentially and ultimately beauty of the soul. St. Augustine gave this advice:

It is well that He seeks your beauty within [your heart], where He has given you the power to become daughters of God. He does not seek from you a fair body but fair conduct, by which you control your body too. He is not the kind to whom one can tell a lie about you, and make Him jealous and angry. See with how great security you love Him, whom you do not fear to offend by false suspicions. Husband and wife love each other, because they see each other; and what they do not see, they are fearful of in regard to each other. Nor is their delight in what can be seen sure. And in matters that are hidden they usually suspect what does not exist. You have nothing to blame in Him nor do you fear lest by what is false you haply offend Him, whom you do not see with the eyes but behold by faith. (*On Holy Virginity*, n. 55)[44]

The high priest and the ancients of Israel praised Judith's chaste widowhood and valor. Their words might be adapted to everyone who lives in perfect chastity:

You are the glory of Jerusalem, you are the joy of Israel, you are the honor of our people. For you have done manfully, and your heart has been strengthened, because you have loved chastity, and after your husband you have not known any other. Therefore also the hand of the Lord has strengthened you, and therefore you shall be blessed forever. (Judith 15,10-11)

In one of his special visions John the Apostle saw a great sign in heaven: "A woman clothed with the sun, and the moon under her feet, and a crown of twelve stars on her head" (Apocalypse 12,1). That is, according to Pope Saint Pius X, the Blessed Virgin Mother of Christ in glory, as Virgin Mother of Christ and of all Christians (Encyclical *Ad diem illum*, Feb. 2, 1904).[45] As Mother of all Christians, however, Mary is here the exemplar and incorporation of the Church, the Virgin Mother of all Christians and the Spouse of Christ. Since the virgin and chaste brides of Christ are such in imitation of the Virgin Mother Mary and the Virgin Mother Church, one can readily and correctly accommodate this Apocalyptic picture of Mary and the Church to every bride of Christ. For every bride of Jesus is adorned with the sun of His grace; she is crowned with the glory and honor of all her good works. She, in other words, shares in the beauty of Mary and the Church, both virgin mothers.

Perfect chastity is truly the white lily among the virtues. It is the perennial springtime of God's kingdom on earth. That is why, borrowing from the Canticle of love in the Old Covenant, the Church sings in her solemn Consecration of Virgins:

Be espoused, my beloved, and come, the winter is past, the turtledove is singing, the vineyards, in full bloom, give off their fragrance.

If virginity and perfect chastity are all that—and they are—then they must give immense glory to God. God's glory is the primary and ultimate reason for the existence of any created being or act. It must, then, be the primary and ultimate reason for perfect chastity. Perfect chastity is the incense that is offered on the altars of virginal and chaste hearts and that ascends heavenward as sweet and pleasant fragrance, to the very throne of Christ and God, giving delight to them. It is one of the choicest flowers in God's garden and radiates a most pleasant perfume, which delights God exceedingly. He seems to have manifested that delight by allowing a number of the bodies of chaste Saints to give off a very special fragrance after death.

In a special way virginal and chaste love is a manifestation, a revelation, of the glories of Christ the Spouse. It is a profession of faith in the mystery of Christ's redemption and death and resurrection, in which Christ's brides proclaim their faith and their love, in which they share most abundantly.

Let us conclude this section with the exclamation of the great St. Paul: "Eye has not seen nor ear heard, nor has it entered into the heart of man, what things God has prepared for those who love him" (1 Corinthians 2,9) in perfect chastity.

CHAPTER NINE

For Whom Is This Vocation?

TO LIVE A SINGLE LIFE IN THE WORLD IN PERFECT CHASTITY and deliberately to will to do so for a lifetime out of love for Christ is a distinct grace of God. It is, in the strict sense of the word, a vocation. One must be called to it by God. God must give one this great gift. Ordinarily God gives His call in a silent manner. Certainly, one should not wait for a loud voice of God thundering that He is calling one to this form of life. God usually gives His grace and call by making a person fit to live this type of life and by inspiring the correct motives for choosing it, and, at times, by allowing circumstances that will hinder one from choosing any other vocation.

As we described earlier, one must make a free and deliberate choice of this type of life. The choice can still be free, even when circumstances conspire against choosing any other vocation. If one would like to have married but must remain unmarried because of circumstances, or if one is prevented for various reasons from entering the priesthood or the religious life, one may, and should, make the best of circumstances and freely consent to live in perfect chastity, since that is God's will.

In other cases, namely, when one would be free to choose one of the other vocations, but freely chooses to serve God in single perfect chastity, one must have the proper motives. One should have a well-balanced attitude toward life and toward the other vocations. All vocations are good, coming as they do from the all-wise and all-holy God, and leading back to Him. One may not choose to live the single life merely because one has a false notion that marriage is a necessary evil and that sex is ugly, or that married persons are but second rate Christians, or even because there are too many trials in married life, or because one is too selfish to be of service to others, or because one proudly thinks oneself too good for a modern husband or wife. Nor is this vocation for "exhibitionists," for those whose main aim in life is to parade before others and make an impression on them.

The highest motive, of course, for choosing this form of life is the undivided love that one wishes to bestow on Christ and the more perfect union with Christ that one wishes to enjoy even in this life. That amounts to desiring the greater honor and glory of God. In other words, one freely wills perfect and perpetual chastity directly and expressly for its own sake. This motive is not only the highest but also the essential motive for distinguishing such a life from that of a single person in the world who might, for all that, be doing very much good, but who lives in the unmarried state very regretfully. One may, however, and even should, choose the single life in the world, secondarily, for the supernatural motive of charity toward fellow men, since it frees one for a wholehearted devotion to the service of the Church and humanity. For that reason some one has suggested that this vocation is excellent for all who wish to spend their lives in the public service of others: for diplomats and politicians, for lawyers, doctors and teachers. I am not suggesting that all who follow any of these professions must or should remain single. I merely mention that the single state of perfect chastity in the world can be an excellent asset for any one in such a profession of public service.

This vocation, I should like to repeat, may be chosen even though one is not forced to stay out of the other vocations. It should, in fact, be a vocation primarily for those normal and psychically sound people who deliberately choose it in preference to the other vocations, because they feel that this is where God desires that they fulfill His all-holy will. That holds, too, for those who because of nervous illness or other handicaps are not eligible for the religious life or the priesthood, who could, however, choose the married state if they so desired, but who wish to live the more perfect life in the world as spouses of Christ.

In presenting this vocation of perfect chastity in this light, we by no means underestimate the dignity or the need of the priesthood or of the religious life. We realize full well that there is a great need of these vocations especially today, and that those whom God calls to these vocations should be generous, and in a spirit of sacrifice answer His call. But we realize, too, that God gives the vocation of perfect chastity in the world in our day as well as in any other age, and that people to whom He gives it have the right to live by it.

This form of life should not be chosen too early or too late. If chosen too early one may later regret not having chosen one of the other vocations, especially marriage. I say "especially marriage," because it is easy enough to change from the state of perfect chastity in the world to religious life or the priesthood. If one chooses this vocation too late, one might regret having lost so much valuable time for living a higher form of life, which is more meritorious for eternal glory. Women, in particular, often complain about not having known of this great ideal soon enough. Fresh flowers, not merely those that are withering, should be presented to Christ.

The range of years in which one may choose this vocation is considerable. Spiritual guides put it down as approximately from twenty-five years of age till forty. One might say that about twenty-five is ordinarily not too early for a person to make up his mind on the matter, and after that age it can be chosen any time, the sooner the better. Of course, particular circumstances may make it possible to come to a definite decision while still in one's teens; for instance, if one is a cripple, or one has an incurable sickness that will make the choice of any other vocation impossible or undesirable. And there are certainly chosen souls in every age of Christianity whom God selects for Himself at an earlier age. Often such elect souls think at first that they are called to the religious life; but, on finding this is not the life for them, they settle for the single life in the world. We have the well-known examples of saints like Gemma Galgani, and the recent saintly Edel Quinn, the apostle of the Legion of Mary.

In any case, when first the idea occurs to the mind about following such a vocation, one should give it serious thought. Deliberate the pros and cons for yourself in this vocation as well as in the others. Consult with your spiritual director, usually your ordinary confessor.

Engage in earnest prayer for a time. Try to develop your companionship with the sainted men and women who lived such a life, especially however with St. Joseph and the Blessed Mother and Jesus. Interest yourself in some acts of self-denial as the proper seasoning for earnest prayer. Constantly develop a greater spirit of detachment from worldly pleasures. Try to live more and more in communion with Christ, who would like to be your Spouse, and with the Most Holy Trinity that dwells in your soul through grace as your most intimate Friend. Make constant effort to improve your character, especially along the lines of the essential Christian virtues: faith, hope, charity, humility, fortitude, patience, a spirit of poverty, and, of course modesty and purity. In that spirit abide the time to make your definitive choice.

When you are old enough to make the definitive choice, make a novena of prayers and spiritual exercises that you may really know God's will in the matter. Make a retreat if possible. It goes without saying that you will again ask the advice of your confessor or some other spiritual director who knows you well enough to advise you properly.

St. Paul encouraged widows to remain single. He did not consider it sinful for a person to marry again after the death of the first spouse. Not at all. He deemed it more meritorious, though, for widows to live in single chastity, for the same reasons that he gave for virgins: a more undivided love of Christ and a more undistracted service of fellow men. Listen to his words to the Corinthians:

But I say to the unmarried and to widows, it is good for them if they so remain, even as I. But if they do not have self-control, let them marry, for it is better to marry than to burn. . . . A woman is bound as long as her husband is alive, but if her husband dies, she is free. Let her marry whom she pleases, only let it be in the Lord. But she will be more blessed, in my judgment, if she remains as she is. (1 Corinthians 7,8;40)

In his first letter to Timothy, when counselling widows, St. Paul manifests that he considers their lot a happy one, inasmuch as they can devote themselves to God's service more fully: "But she who is truly a widow, and left solitary, has set her hope on God and continues in supplications and prayers night and day" (1 Timothy 5,5).

Widows, and all this holds equally for widowers, can deliberately forego any future marriage and live in perfect chastity for the remainder of their lives for the "kingdom of heaven's sake." Then they will fall under the category of those who practice perfect chastity, though not in the complete sense of those who never married and always remained virgins. Pope Pius XII distinctly speaks of "perfect chastity," apart from virginity, because later he expressly notes that his letter is meant for "all those beloved sons and daughters who in any way have consecrated their bodies and souls to God" (*On Holy Virginity*, p. 163). Prior to that he had singled out widows and widowers among the "innumerable . . . multitude of those who from the beginnings of the Church until our time have offered their chastity to God. . . . Others, upon the death of their spouse, have consecrated to God perpetual widowhood" (p. 162). These too will merit immensely, because, although corporal integrity is a great gift, chastity is essentially a spiritual gift, an interior virtue of the will.

In the ancient Church, widows who lived a chaste life were respected in a special way, as can be seen from Paul's letters. The Churchmen, too, wrote in defense of chaste widowhood, insisting that it was of greater dignity than marriage, though a second marriage was in no way sinful. Often they wrote an entire treatise on widowhood. St. Augustine, for instance, gives this advice:

The good of widowed continence is, therefore, becoming in a brighter fashion, since in order to vow and profess it, women disregard what both gives pleasure and is lawful. Though after the profession of a vow, one must perseveringly restrain and overcome what gives pleasure, since it is no longer lawful. (*On*

Widowhood, Ch. 11, n. 14)[46] Both by certain reason and by the authority of the Sacred Scriptures, we find that marriage is not a sin, and yet we do not make it equal, to the good of either virginal or widowed chastity. (*On Holy Virginity*, Ch. 19, n. 19)[47] We, however, according to the faith and sound doctrine of Sacred Scripture, say that marriage is no sin, and yet place its good not only below virginal but also below widowed continence, and say that the present necessity of the married hinders their merit, not indeed with respect to eternal life, but with respect to an excellent glory and honor, which is reserved for perpetual continence, and that at this time marriage is not expedient except for such as cannot be continent. . . . (*On Holy Virginity*, Ch. 21, n. 21)[48]

The widows, too, if they have vowed perfect chastity, are brides of Christ. St. Augustine is again to the point:

For, previously, when they were subject to and faithfully served their own husbands, they used to have Him, not as a carnal but as a spiritual Spouse, whose life is the Church herself, of whom they are members, who by integrity of faith, hope, charity, is totally a virgin, not only in sacred virgins, but in widows, too, and in the faithful married women. (*On Widowhood*, Ch. 10, n. 13)[49]

He also advises widows: "With genuine affection and holiest chastity, love to be loved by such a Spouse" (*On Widowhood*, n. 23).[50] He encouraged not only such as already thought about remaining widows, but advised perfect chastity for such as had been thinking about a second marriage: "Still I see that I must say such things as will lead those, too, who had till now thought of marriage to love it and lay hold of it [widowhood]," because that, as he explains, is pleasing to God, since they can give Him a more undivided service (*Ibid.*).[51]

In the history of the Church there have been innumerable widows and widowers who in that single state strove for greater perfection. Many of them have been beatified and canonized. Outstanding examples are St. Elizabeth of Hungary and St. Elizabeth of Portugal.

Again, a life of perfect chastity, willed deliberately, can be advised to the following class of people. It happens, all too frequently in our day, that one's spouse has separated permanently, and conditions exist which make re-union impossible (for instance, attempted marriage from which children were born). The other spouse is thus stranded, bound by a valid marriage but forced to live a single life. Such a one can make his or her very unfortunate situation and severe trial not only bearable but a great blessing by deliberately offering the sacrifice of perfect chastity to Christ for His greater honor and glory and for the spouse's own untold merit of grace and glory. Faith and hope will make this chaste love a glorious thing.

Further, similar advice can be given to those who have been deflowered against their will and perhaps have a child but cannot find a partner for lawful marriage. Their lot can be strewn with many flowers of joy and peace if they realize that they are able to devote their single life in perfect chastity for the love of Christ and in the service of humanity, especially in behalf of the more unfortunate people of our race.

Lastly, there are those who have deliberately sinned, perhaps often, against the holy virtue of purity, but have not gotten married and do not intend to, or maybe can no longer find a partner. Such unfortunate people can, when they come to repentance, dedicate their future to Christ in holy and repentant chastity. For them this will be paradise regained. Pius XII expressly mentions such among the "innumerable . . . multitudes of those who from the beginnings of the Church until our time have offered their chastity to God . . . ; finally, [those who] after repenting of their sins, have chosen a life of perfect chastity" (*On Holy Virginity*, p. 162).

The history of the Church, here too, can boast of many a saintly and sainted man and woman who regained paradise in this fashion. There is the proto-penitent St. Mary Magdalene, whom Christ Himself converted to such a life. Her feast is celebrated as that of a "penitent," but there are passages in her liturgy that look upon her as Christ's bride. There remains some of the ideal of virginal love that even penitents can desire and merit. Another classic example is St. Margaret of Cortona, the Franciscan Tertiary. She had lived a very sinful life with her fiancé, until she found him in a ditch, murdered. The sight of him changed her life. She became the penitent Margaret. Later, in a vision, we are told, Christ called her His friend, child, daughter, and even beloved spouse, and He assured her that her place in heaven would be among the virgins, whose glory she would share. There is also the late Parisian actress, the saintly Eva Lavallière, who forsook the stage and her sinful life when she was at the height of her glory, and devoted herself to years of heroic penance.

St. Thomas teaches that chastity can be regained by contrition and penance. The reason is that chastity is essentially a virtue of the will, and so the violation of chastity can be repaired by opposite acts of the will, by a firm will to live a chaste life in the future (cf. *Summa Theologica*, Part 2-2, q. 152, a. 3).

Chapter Ten

Jesus and Mary and Virginal Chastity

WE HAVE FREQUENTLY REFERRED TO JESUS CHRIST AND HIS relation to virginity and perfect chastity. It seems worth while to gather here into one picture Our Lord's relation to this flower of Christianity.

Christ is a virgin, *the* Virgin, in fact. He is the most perfect Virgin of all times. He lived a life of perfect chastity, and lived it with the greatest possible perfection. No mere creature, not even the Blessed Ever-Virgin Mother of His, could ever equal, much less surpass, the perfection of His virtue of virginal chastity. That is why in the hymn of Vespers for Virgins we sing of Him as the "Crown of virgins." For that reason, too, He is the King of virgins. St. Methodius styles Him beautifully "the Chief-Virgin," just as "the Chief-Priest" and "the Chief-Prophet"; he also calls Him "the leader of the choir of virgins." (*The Banquet of the Ten Virgins*, Discourse 1, Ch. 4 and 5)[52]

Jesus, in His very origin and entire life on earth, was most intimately associated with virginal persons. As Divine Word He chose His own mother, the Virgin Mother, who conceived Him in a virginal manner and gave birth to Him without detriment to her virginity, who remained a perfect virgin ever after. She is the Ever-Virgin.

Virginity, then, by divine design, is strictly united with motherhood in the Incarnation of Jesus. Mary was totally and perpetually consecrated to God by virginity. Her title is The Virgin, by which she was known already in the second century. From the first moment of her conception, she was the Immaculate, and always free from ill-ordered passions. She kept her chaste soul untarnished forever. It is commonly believed, and rightly, that Mary had made a vow of virginity early in life, and that she implies so much in her question to the angel at the Annunciation: "How shall this be, since I do not know man?" (Luke 1,34).

Though Christ is, in a sense, *the* Author of virginity, inasmuch as He is the Redeemer of the grace of virginity and the brightest Exemplar of virgins, nevertheless, Mary is author of virginity prior to Christ, inasmuch as she, the Virgin Mother, gave birth to Christ. Pope Pius XII writes on this matter: "Already Athanasius calls attention to the fact that virginity has its origin in Mary,[53] and Augustine, too, clearly teaches the same thing by these words: 'Virginal dignity began with the Lord's Mother' "[54] (*On Holy Virginity*, p. 188).

Not only was Jesus' Mother a virgin, but His father, Joseph, was a virgin; in fact, His peculiar title would seem to be Virgin Father of Jesus. It is a matter of faith that he had no part in the conception of Jesus, and that he had no other children by Mary. Today it is commonly held that he had no children by any supposed previous marriage. In fact, outstanding theologians maintain that, like Mary, he had made a firm resolve of virginity already prior to their marriage, which was virginal.[55]

For His herald, the Savior of the world chose a virgin

soul, St. John the Baptist. It was John's office, as friend of the Bridegroom, to prepare the way for the Bridegroom, Jesus, and to bear witness to Him (cf. John 3,29). That work done, he sealed his virginal life by martyrdom, and thus testified to the Messias also by his death.

Another John, the beloved disciple, the most intimate confidant of Christ, was a virgin. He rested on the bosom of the Lord at the Last Supper (John 13,23). He was deserving of this greater manifestation of loving intimacy, because of his virginal chastity. It was to this pure virgin that Our Lord entrusted His Ever-Virgin Mother just before dying on the cross. It was he, too, who merited at that cross to represent all mankind as children of the Virgin Mother of God (John 19,26-27).

It is plain, then, that Jesus Christ desired virginal souls not only in His Church but in closest relation to the essential mysteries of the Incarnation and Redemption. He desired, moreover, that virginal souls continue to do honor to and grace His Church. He established in His Church the new mode of life of perfect chastity and virginity. He is the author of this mode of life by His shining example and counsel. It is from the lips of Christ Himself that the Church has received her knowledge of and interest in virginal and perfect chastity. Pope Pius XII words this concisely:

In point of fact, when the obligations and inconveniences of marriage, which their Master had brought to light in His discourse, seemed very burdensome to the disciples, and when they had said to Him: "If the case of a man with his wife is so, it is not expedient to marry" (Matthew 19,12), Jesus Christ replied that not all can grasp that saying, but only those to whom that [gift] has been given. As He explained, some people are impeded from marriage by a defect of nature, others by the

violence and wickedness of men; but others abstain from it by
their own free will, and that, "for the kingdom of heaven's sake"
(Matthew 19,12). He concluded with these words: "Let him
accept it who can." (*On Holy Virginity*, p. 164)

The fact that Christ did not speak more frequently on this
subject is no argument against its truth or importance in
His mind. He expressed Himself on the matter once for all
time. He was just as divine and infallible that one time as
for any other truth. Christ is, therefore, the Author of Virginity and perfect chastity as a recognized and honorable
mode of life in His Church. Indirectly, at least, He extolled
this form of life when, arguing against the Pharisees, He
insisted that in heaven there will be no marriages or married life; there all people will live like the angels (Matthew
22,30). In other words, He meant that this form of life,
which is heavenly and angelic, is the more perfect. The
Churchmen have so understood Christ and have used His
statement to illustrate the life of virgins already on earth.

Christ's final relation to virginity and perfect chastity is
that He is the end of this virtue as well as of all virtues. We
must practice it for Christ's glory and honor. In turn, for
having practiced it faithfully, Christ will be our eternal
reward, our glory.

We have spoken already of Mary's relation to virginity
inasmuch as she was associated with Christ and His circle
of virginal souls. More must now be said about her and her
relation to virginal and perfect chastity in Christians. Mary
was virgin not only physically by integrity of body, but also
interiorly by the inner virtue of chastity and virginity. She
practiced virginal chastity with full deliberation. She even
sealed her proposal of virginity with a vow, as has been the
constant mind of the Church. In that she is the teacher and

model of virginity and perfect chastity for all Christians who would live such a life under vow. Quoting from the Fathers, Pope Pius XII nicely sums up Mary's being Model of virgins:

And following in the footsteps of Athanasius,[56] Ambrose proposes the Virgin Mary's life as the pattern for virgins: "Imitate her, my daughters.[57] Mary's life should be for you as a portrayal of virginity, from which as from a mirror is reflected the loveliness of chastity and the beauty of virtue. From it you should take lessons of living, where instructions for upright living are expressed as in a model that show what you ought to correct, what to imitate, what to retain . . . This is the picture of virginity. For Mary was such that her life alone is a lesson for all.[58] Holy Mary, therefore, should describe the instruction of [your] life.[59] Her grace was so great that not only did she preserve the grace of virginity in herself, but she also bestowed the honor of integrity on those on whom she gazed." [60] How true is not this expression of Ambrose: "O the riches of Mary's virginity." [61] Of a truth, because of these riches it is of greatest value for today's virgins and religious men and women to contemplate Mary's virginity, that they may practice the chastity of their own state more faithfully and more perfectly. (*On Holy Virginity*, p. 188)

Mary's virginity, together with her motherhood, was most fruitful physically in that she conceived and gave birth to the Divine Redeemer. But Mary's virginity and motherhood are fruitful spiritually too. She is the spiritual Mother of all Christians, and she is so as a Virgin. In her sacred womb she conceived virginally not only the Head of the Mystical Body, as Pope St. Pius X stated in his encyclical *Ad diem illum*, but the entire Mystical Body as well.[62] At the cross, when she cooperated further in the spiritual regeneration of mankind, she was declared by Christ to be the Mother of all men, represented by the virgin disciple (John 19,26-27). John, at that moment, represented all men who would be children of Mary, but he represented in a special way those who would be virginal children of Mary by living in perfect chastity for a lifetime, as he was doing. In a very special way these would be Mary's children, and she would be their Virgin Mother.

Again, Mary as Virgin Mother is the teacher and model of all virgins. She shows them the way to make their virginal lives fruitful for God. We touched on this before: how virgins are truly mothers in the spiritual order, by helping to beget and rear children spiritually for eternal life in heaven. Their model in this is the Virgin Mother of Jesus and of all Christians. Sister Mary St. Virginia, in a poem entitled *A Nun to Mary, Virgin*,[63] has expressed this truth in lyric lines:

> I had gone fruitless and defenceless, Lady,
> Had it not been for your strange blossoming:
> Out of the sun and rain, in still and shady
> And lonely moorlands, uncaressed by wing,
> My having life had been a thing to mourn for,
> Passing none on nor yielding up perfume—
> Without you I had cringed beneath a corn for
> Skylarks that soar not, trees that do not bloom.
> Without you I had had no answer to
> The jibe against my love and my sweet mating—
> Now, as I reach to take a Child from you,
> These lips send far beyond my cloister grating
> The canticle a million maids have cried,
> Finding in you themselves: and justified.

Mary, like Jesus, is the crown of virgins, because she is the most perfect Virgin, and to her all other virgins must give glory. She is the Queen of virgins; they all must do her honor by offering to her praise and glory with the perfume of their virginal and chaste lives. She is the Virgin of virgins. All virgins will be her glory, her crown of stars, forever in heaven; she in turn will be their glory, shedding light and love and joy on them from her glorified self.

CHAPTER ELEVEN

Virginal Chastity and the Virgin Church

AT THE ANNUNCIATION OR INCARNATION A SOLEMN NUPTIAL was ratified between the Word of God and the Church. The Virgin Mary was the representative of the Church; and in the name of the Church, and in a sense as the embodiment of the Church, she gave consent to the Incarnation, to the nuptials between the Divine Word and His Church. That is the teaching of the Popes, who quote St. Thomas and crystallize an ancient tradition. In his encyclical on the Mystical Body, Pope Pius XII expresses it thus:

> Her most holy soul was filled with the Divine Spirit of Jesus Christ more than all other souls created by God. And "in place of the entire human nature," she gave her consent that there might be "a kind of spiritual nuptials between the Son of God and human nature" (St. Thomas, *Summa Theologica*, Part 3, q. 80, a. 1). It was in her virginal womb that Christ Our Lord was already adorned with the dignity of Head of the Church, to whom as Fountain of all heavenly life, she then gave birth by a wonderful child-bearing.[63a]

The Pope speaks of nuptials between God's Son and human nature, because the union of God's Son with human nature in Christ Himself was a marriage. It is, in fact, the exemplar of the union between Christ and the Church, which it made possible, and which it included, since Christ in assuming an individual human nature assumed all human nature in order to save it and make it part of His Mystical Body.

This doctrine is contained in St. Paul. In his letter to the Ephesians, 5,23-32, quoted earlier, he writes that Christ loved the Church as His Bride, and that the union between Christ and the Church was foreshadowed by the union of Adam and Eve in matrimonial love. That can mean only this: The union of Christ and His Church is a spiritual bridal union for the sake of begetting children of God. This idea underlies the doctrine of the Churchmen from ancient times that the Church was born from the wounded side of the Savior on the cross, just as Eve was formed from the side of Adam; see Genesis 2,23-24.

That Christ's Church would be His bride and our Mother was foreshadowed in the Old Testament by the fact that the true Israel of the Old Covenant was God's bride and a virgin mother, according to the teaching of the prophets. Isaias, for instance, preached:

Give praise and make joyful noise, you that did not travail with child; for many are the children of the desolate, more than of her that has a husband, says the Lord." (Isaias 54,1)

Ezechiel describes graphically how God wooed Israel when she was poor and dirty, how He cleansed, enriched, and beautified her with dresses and jewels. But Israel became an unfaithful spouse, a harlot and adulteress, inasmuch as she courted the pagan religions (Ezechiel 16,6-63). It was, in fact, the covenant with Israel through Abraham that was thought of as the espousal of God with His Chosen Nation (Ezechiel 16,8). The prophets, under divine inspiration, often referred to Israel's unfaithfulness to God as a sin of fornication or adultery, in a metaphorical sense and in the spiritual order. See especially Osee 1-3, where the prophet describes the long patience of God with His unfaithful spouse. See also Isaias 50,1; Jeremias 13,27; Ezechiel 23,43.

The Canticle of Canticles, in particular, describes God's relation to Israel as one of a bridegroom toward a bride. The same is true of Psalm 44. But here we cross already, in prophecy, to the true Israel of the New Covenant, because the King and His Queen of this Psalm are the Messias and His Church. So for the New Israel it is no longer God as such that is the Spouse, but God's Son.

That Christ has a spouse is implied in John 3,29-30, where John the Baptist refers to himself as the friend of the Bridegroom, who is Christ. In fact, Christ refers to Himself as a Bridegroom, who is celebrating a wedding feast in this world (cf. Mark 2,19-20). It is, then, not without deeper implications that Christ used the figure of a wedding feast to describe in parable various facets of truth about His Church (cf. Matthew 25,1-13; 22,1-14).

Our Lord revealed to John that the Church is a beautiful heavenly bride all adorned for the nuptial feast (Apocalypse 19,7-9; 21,9-10). That this bride is a virgin is clear from the fact that her spouse is the God-Man and the union is entirely spiritual, for the spiritual regeneration of souls. That the Church is a virgin mother is implied in the vision of the glorious woman of Chapter 12, whose children are the believers in Christ (cf. vs. 17). This woman is Mary as the Exemplar and incorporation of the Church. She is the Virgin Mother of the Messias (vs. 5) and of all Christians (vs. 17). So the Church, too, is a Virgin Mother.

With this basis in Scripture it is not surprising that the Church Fathers should have developed the doctrine of the

Church's being not only our Mother but our Virgin Mother and Christ's Bride. A few quotations from them will impress this fact on our minds. Clement of Jerusalem wrote:

> O mystic marvel! One is the Father of all things, one, too, the Word of all things, and one the Holy Spirit, who is the same everywhere. One only is the Virgin Mother. To call her Church is dear to me. This Mother alone has no milk, since she alone did not become a wife; but she is virgin at the same time as mother; immaculate as virgin, loving as mother. . . . [Her Child] is the Body of Christ. (*The Instructor*, Bk. 1, Ch. 6, n. 41)[64]

St. Methodius apostrophizes the Church in these words:

> With hymns we attendants of the Bride honor you, O blessed Bride of God, O undefiled Virgin, Church of snow-white body, dark-haired, chaste, spotless, beloved. (*The Banquet of the Ten Virgins*, Discourse 11, Ch. 2)[65]

Earlier, in Discourse 3, Ch. 8,[66] he had developed at length, with the aid of Genesis 2,22-24 and Ephesians 5,23-32, the idea that the Church is the Bride of the Second Adam, and is most fruitful. Let us note these words:

> Thus, too, the command "Be fruitful and multiply" is duly realized. The Church is fruitful daily in greatness and beauty and multitude by union and communion with the Word, who still comes down to us and falls into ecstacy in the Memorial of His Passion. Otherwise the Church could not conceive believers and give them new birth by the bath of regeneration, unless Christ emptied Himself that He might be contained by them through the recapitulation of His Passion, as I said, and died again, having come down from heaven; and so, having been "united with His wife," the Church, He provides that a certain power is taken from His own side, so that all who are

built up in Him might grow up, those, namely, who are born again by the bath, receiving of His bones and flesh, that is, of His holiness and glory.[67]

St. Ambrose has this to say:

Thus, Holy Church, unstained by sexual intercourse, but fruitful in child-bearing, is a virgin by chastity, a mother by offspring. She, therefore, bears us her children as a virgin, fruitful, not by a man, but by the Spirit. She bears us not with pain of her members, but with the joys of the angels. As Virgin she feeds us, not with the milk of the body, but with the milk of the Apostle (1 Corinthians 3,2), with which he fed the people of tender age, who were still growing up. For what married woman has more children than Holy Church, who is a virgin by her sacraments and a mother to her people, whose fruitfulness even Holy Scripture attests, saying: . . . (Isaias 54,1; Galatians 4,19). Our Mother has no husband, but she has a Spouse, inasmuch as she, whether as the Church among the nations, or the soul in individuals, weds the Word of God as her eternal Spouse, without any loss of purity, free from all injury, full of reason. (*On Virgins*, Ch. 6, n. 31)[68]

St. Augustine, as might be expected, is full of these ideas. Frequently and insistently he touches upon them in his commentary on the Psalms, in his dogmatic treatises, in his catechetical instructions, in his sermons. He has a long treatment in his work *On Holy Virginity*, where he shows the relation between the spiritual motherhood of Mary and of the Church and of Christ's virgin brides. Let us note these words on the fruitfulness of the Church:

And by this, that one woman, not only in spirit but also in body, is both mother and virgin. Mother indeed in spirit, not of our Head, which is the Savior Himself, of whom rather she was born spiritually, inasmuch as all who have believed in

Him, among whom she too is, are rightly called "the children of the Bridegroom" (Matthew 9,15). She is, however, certainly mother of His members, which we are, because she cooperated by charity that the faithful should be born in the Church, who are members of that Head. But in body she is mother of the Head Himself. For it behooved that our Head, by a singular miracle, should be born of a virgin according to the flesh, that by this He might signify that His members would be born of the Virgin Church according to the spirit. Therefore, Mary alone both in spirit and in body is mother and virgin: both Mother of Christ and Virgin of Christ. The Church, however, in the saints who will possess God's kingdom is indeed in spirit totally mother of Christ and totally Virgin of Christ; in body, however, not totally, but in certain ones she is virgin of Christ, in certain others, mother but not of Christ. Of course, both faithful women who are married and virgins dedicated to God are mothers of Christ spiritually by holy conduct and "charity from a pure heart and a good conscience and faith unfeigned" (1 Timothy 1,5), inasmuch as they do the Father's will (n. 6).[69]

Christ, then, and the Church, His Virgin Bride, beget children for the supernatural life through the power of the Holy Spirit, in imitation of the virginal conception and birth of Christ Himself from the Virgin Mary through the power of the Holy Spirit, and, more directly, in imitation of Mary's spiritual, virginal motherhood of all Christians.

Virginal bridal love is, therefore, intimately associated with the deepest mysteries of salvation. It is into this picture of bridal love of Christ and His Virgin Mother, Mary, and His Virgin Church that the bridal love of virginal and perfect chastity is to be set. It is from Christ and the Church that the soul receives the power to live such a virginal life, to be a virginal child of God and consecrate his or her entire life to Christ in perfect chastity. It is according to the pattern of the Virgin Bride, the Church, that any virgin soul becomes spiritually fruitful. In union with Christ and through the power of His grace the virgin soul becomes fruitful in working for the edification of Christ's Mystical Body, of Christ's very own Bride. The Church is, therefore, not only the exemplar of the virgin and chaste person, she is also the end, the final cause of such a soul's life, inasmuch as the virgin soul works for the glory of the Church and of Christ. Virgin and chaste souls, consequently, show forth by their lives the perfect virgin motherhood of the Church, as Pope Pius XII wrote so nicely:

We should like to make a special reflection on the following most pleasant fruit of virginity: the consecrated virgins make manifest and, as it were, place before our eyes the perfect virginity of our Mother the Church herself, as well as the holiness of their own very intimate union with Christ. Precisely for that reason the words were wisely written which the Bishop who performs the rite of consecration of virgins, uses and humbly prays to God: ". . . there should exist more lofty-minded souls, who would disdain the marriage that consists in bodily union of man and wife, and would long for the mystery [that it foreshadows], and would not imitate what *is done* in nuptials, but would love what *is signified* by the nuptials." (*On Holy Virginity*, p. 173)

In fact, the Pope calls this their greatest dignity, to be the radiant reflection of the virginal integrity of their Holy Mother Church, as the Bride of Christ:

The fact that virgins are the living images of the perfect integrity, by which the Church is united with her Divine Spouse, is without doubt the greatest glory of virgins. And the fact that these same virgins are a wonderful sign of the flourishing holiness and of that spiritual fruitfulness, in which the society founded by Jesus Christ excels, certainly brings to this society a joy that is most ardent. About this Cyprian wrote very well: "These are the well-known flower of the Church's offspring, the glory and the ornament of spiritual grace, the joyful personalities, the intact and incorrupt work [worthy] of praise and honor, the image of God that is like the Lord's holiness, the more illustrious portion of Christ's flock. Through them the glorious fruitfulness of Mother Church rejoices and in them it flourishes abundantly. And the more virginity, already copious, adds to her numbers, so much the more does the Mother's joy increase." (*On Holy Virginity*, p. 173 f.)[70]

That virgin souls are spiritually fruitful in imitation of their Virgin Mother the Church is clearly taught by many of the Churchmen, often as a continuation of their discourse about the fruitfulness of the Church. It was so in St. Methodius' *The Banquet of the Ten Virgins*, Discourse 3, Ch. 8.[71] So, too, it was in St. Augustine. These words of his are worthy of note:

One must not believe that those who consecrate their virginity to God, though elevated to a very high degree of honor and purity, lack true matrimony, because they enter into nuptials of the universal Church in which the Spouse is Christ. (*Commentary on St. John's Gospel*, Tract 9, n. 2)[72]

On the occasion of the spiritual nuptials of Demetrias, a virgin of noble rank, St. Augustine, addressing her mother, wrote:

In your home so much fruit has arisen that, even though the human nuptials were all prepared, the saintly Demetrias preferred the spiritual embrace of the Spouse who is more beautiful than the sons of men, and whom the virgins wed in order to obtain a more abundant fruitfulness of the spirit, without losing the integrity of the flesh. (Letter n. 188)[73]

We saw above how, in his treatise *On Holy Virginity*, St. Augustine illustrated the greater fruitfulness of spiritual cooperation in making Christians, by supposing that a rich woman buys many slaves in order to have them duly baptized as Christians. A mother, by giving physical birth to a child, does not thereby make it a Christian; she too must see that the child is baptized and made a Christian after birth. That very thing, however, even a virgin bride of Christ, through spiritual motherhood, through the inner acts and the outer works of the apostolate, can do, and often in a more effective and more extensive manner than a real mother. See Augustine's treatise (n. 9).[74]

St. Ambrose sums the matter up concisely as follows:

He [God] even loves in less beautiful bodies the more beautiful souls. Though the burden of the womb and the pangs of childbirth are unknown, more numerous still is the offspring of a pious soul, which considers all as its children, which is fruitful in heirs but barren of all bereavement, which knows no funerals but possesses many heirs. (*On Virgins*, Bk. 1, Ch. 6, n. 30)[75]

The Virgin Church clearly and beautifully manifests her own virginal status precisely and pre-eminently through the virgin souls who choose her as model. Recall the words of Pope Pius XII and his quotation from St. Cyprian. Apropos, too, is the remark of Origen: "The Church flourishes as Christ's true Bride and as Virgin with the flowers of the chaste virgins" (*Commentary on Genesis*, Homily 3, n. 6).[76]

CHAPTER TWELVE

History of Virginal Living in the Church

THE VOCATION OF SINGLE PEOPLE LIVING IN THE WORLD IN perfect chastity is not a fad of the hour. It is as ancient as the Virgin Church herself. As early as the age of the Apostles this mode of living was defended and praised highly. We noted the teaching of St. Paul and the statements of St. John. We saw, too, how Our Lord spoke in favor of it and extended a general invitation to all who were willing and courageous enough to practice it. With that background it was quite natural that many should have chosen to live this form of life and that it should have been defended vigorously against enemy attacks and lauded to the heavens.

In the writings of Ignatius of Antioch, who was martyred A.D. 107, we find that virgins are a special group in the Christian community. He salutes them in his letter to the Smyrneans (Ch. 13, n. 1),[77] and exhorts them to perseverance in his letters to St. Polycarp (Ch. 5, n. 2)[78] and to the Ephesians (Ch. 10, n. 3).[79] St. Polycarp, too, admonishes the virgins, considered as a special class of Christians, to walk with a blameless and chaste conscience.[80]

About the middle of the second century the apologists

arose to defend, among other things, the chaste and virginal living of Christians against the pagan accusations of
immoralities. St. Justin (d. about A.D. 165) could make this
boast:

There are some who have been made eunuchs for the kingdom of heaven's sake; but all cannot accept this saying [namely,
Matthew 19,12] . . . There are many men and many women
who have reached sixty and seventy years of age, who have
been Christ's disciples from childhood, and who remain pure.
I am proud to say that I could produce such from every class of
men. (*Apology* I, Ch. 15)[81]

Athenagoras of Athens, addressing himself to the Emperor Marcus Aurelius Antonius and his son, L. Aurelius
Commodus, defended Christian living against pagan attacks.
Christians were not only not guilty of the immoralities of
which pagans accused them, but they were careful to practice purity of thought as well as of deeds. He too boasted,
rightly: "Why, you would find among us, both men and
women, growing old unmarried, in the hope of living in
closer communion with God" (*A Plea for Christians*, Ch.
33).[82] Likewise, Theophilus, Bishop of Antioch, who died
after 181, defends the innocence of the Christians, and in-
forms us that they observe continence as well as chastity.[83]

Beginning with the third century, we have longer passages
and even entire treatises in praise and defense of chastity
and virginity. These treatises form a special category of excellent Christian literature. Tertullian (d. after 220) is the
first on record to write a treatise exclusively on the exalted
nature of continence, *To His Wife*, in which he encourages
his wife, after his death, to forego a second marriage in the
higher interests of the soul. He treated the matter of virginity and modesty in his *On Veiling Virgins*. He touched
upon the problem also in other works, some of which are,

however, infected with Montanism. His compatriot, St. Cyprian (d. 250), composed a pastoral sermon *On the Apparel of Virgins,* which has lost none of its vitality through all the centuries.

St. Ambrose (d. 397) is considered the apostle of virginity in the Western Church. He composed several treatises on the subject. In 377 he wrote *On Virgins, to His Sister Marcellina,* which consists of three parts: the first is on the excellence of virginity, the second is a group of tableaux of heroines of this form of life, the third gives norms for living as Christ's spouse. That same year he wrote the work *On Widows.* A year later he composed *On Virginity,* which is more apologetic in tone. In 391-2 he penned *On the Virgin and on the Perpetual Virginity of Holy Mary,* because in Mary is realized the supreme model of feminine purity. The next year he produced another precious work, *An Exhortation on Virginity.*

St. Jerome (d. 420) defended the perpetual virginity of Mary in a work *Against Helvidius* (A.D. 383), and virginity in general in *Against Jovinian,* in two books (A.D. 393), where, however, he somewhat exaggerates the excellence of virginity. In *Against Vigilantius* he defended clerical celibacy (A.D. 406). He proved himself an able and energetic counsellor to virgins and wrote a number of letters to that effect. Well-known are the letters to the virgins Eustochius (A.D. 384) and Demetrias (A.D. 414).

When St. Augustine came on the scene (d. 430), the practical side of this problem had been taken care of rather well. He could, therefore, devote himself more to the development of the mystical ideal of virginal life, and its relation to the Virgin Church. His main work is *On Holy Virginity* (A.D. 401). Three other works have considerable material on the same subject: *On Continence* (A.D. 395), *On the Good of Matrimony* (A.D. 401), *On the Good of*

Widowhood (A.D. 414). Besides these treatises, he has pertinent passages in many of his other writings.

Niceta of Remesiana (d. after 414) is today recognized as author of *On the Fallen Virgin,* which had been ascribed to St. Ambrose. The last treatise in the Latin Church worth noting is that of St. Leander (d. 601) to his sister Florence: *On the Formation of Virgins and the Contempt of the World.*

In the Eastern Church, sometime in the third century, two letters were written on the virginal life. They had been wrongly ascribed to Pope Clement of Rome, and are often referred to as the Pseudo-Clementine Letters. But they are important for the study of the history of virginity. They denounced the abuse of virgins of both sexes living together, and they demand a high degree of spirituality for virgins.

St. Methodius (d. 311) composed his beautiful *Symposion,* or *The Banquet of the Ten Virgins,* along classical lines. Ten virgins one after the other sing the praise of virginity. At the end St. Thecla sings a hymn of praise for Christ as Spouse of the Church.

From the early Alexandrian school we have no treatise on the subject, even though in the nearby deserts the hermitic life flourished. But Clement of Alexandria (d. before 215), though he extolled the conjugal state very highly, was aware of the more perfect state of virginity. Origen composed no special treatise on chastity or virginity, yet he wrote so well on the topic in many places of his works that if these were all gathered into one work, they would make one of the finest works in the literature on virginity. St. Athanasius (d. 373), who while in exile had been able to observe the heroic virtue of the monks in the desert, and subsequently composed *The Life of St. Anthony,* also wrote sometime between 350 and 360 a work *On Virginity,* which is a real treasury of counsels for virgin souls.

St. Basil the Great (d. 379) wrote *On the Fallen Virgin,* in which he treats especially the dangers in virginal life. His brother, St. Gregory of Nyssa (d. about 390) also wrote *On Virginity* (about 370), but more from a mystical approach. He likewise has excellent material on the subject in his commentary on Canticles, and in a letter to his sister St. Macrina. (It is interesting to note how many times the virginal life of a sister seems to have occasioned a treatise on the subject by a brother.)

St. John Chrysostom (d. 407) was the apostle of virginity in the East, as St. Ambrose was in the West. He is known especially for his treatise *On Virginity* (after A.D. 376), which is a masterful explanation of 1 Corinthians 7. He also wrote two works for widows (A.D. 380). *To a Young Widow* was meant as a consolation to one who became a widow after only five years of married life. The second work was *On Not Entering a Second Marriage.* Two more works attack the abuse of bachelors and virgins living in common (perhaps A.D. 379).

Some of the ancient Christian poets also sang the praises of virginal chastity. Worthy of mention are: St. Ephraem of Edessa, St. Gregory Nazianzen (who wrote six compositions on virginity: the first is 732 hexameters), Pope St. Damasus (who made some epigrams), St. Avitus (who wrote his poem of 666 hexameters to his sister, Fuscina, a consecrated virgin), and Venantius Fortunatus.

This literature of the early Churchmen was later augmented by the erudite commentaries of the great Scholastics—for instance, St. Thomas Aquinas and St. Bonaventure. Other masters of the spiritual life, too, added their beautiful bouquets of praise and delicious fruits of practical counsels to this ideal of the Christian spiritual life.

The praises of virginity as found in the Churchmen were beautifully mirrored in the Church's prayers, particularly in her Office for such classical Saints as Cecilia, Agnes of Rome, Agatha, and Lucy, in which the antiphons and lessons speak with high enthusiasm of virginal chastity. In due time came the ceremonial for the consecration of virgins, especially the more solemn form, which is a veritable mosaic of praise for virginal life dedicated to Christ the eternal Spouse.

Without making this a scientific disquisition on the history of vocations to virginity, I should like to give at least a brief outline of the matter. This should, I believe, prove to be a powerful incentive for others to follow the footsteps of Christ's heroines and heroes.

Most of the data on individual virgins is on women, since scholars have studied their lives in particular. Besides, the normal vocation for men who wished to live a single life was the priesthood, or the life of hermits or monks. It should not be surprising if the number of lay men who lived a single life in the world was smaller than that of women. And yet we have testimony that men as well as women lived this form of life. As early as the second century, St. Justin, who could speak for the Church from Palestine to Rome, testified that many men and women lived in perfect purity to their sixtieth and seventieth year, and that these came from all social ranks.[84] Athenagoras of Athens, who was acquainted also with Alexandria through his studies, is witness that many, both men and women, grew old in virginity.[85] Tertullian, in his turn, has many exclamatory phrases of "how many" are the voluntary celibates, and "how many" the virgins espoused to Christ.[86] St. Augustine vouches that no one thinks it strange that so many thousands of pure young men and virgins should renounce marriage and observe chastity, although in his time many of these were no doubt religious.[87] Also the Pseudo-Clementine letters of the third century have several references to both men and women, and the first letter is dedicated to both.[88] Their condemning the abuse of both living a common life shows that there were also many men living a celibate life. That men, too, tried to live a celibate life is evident, likewise, from other patristic literature that denounces the abuse of common life for bachelors and virgins.

With Christ and the Apostles highly recommending virginity as a mode of life it is not surprising that already in apostolic times there were people, apart from some of the clergy, who dedicated their lives to virginity. In Acts 21,9 there is the record of the four daughters of the deacon Philip who lived as virgins. In that first century of Christianity we can note these saints who lived as virgins: St. Domitilla (May 12), SS. Euphronsyna and Theodora (May 7), St. Martha of Bethany (July 29), St. Petronilla (May 31), St. Thecla (Sept. 23).

In the second century we have the testimony of St. Ignatius of Antioch, in a letter to the Smyrneans (noted above), that there were a group of virgins at Smyrna. The second century was the age of apologists. But the virgins, the élite of the communities, were the best apologetics for Christ and Christian living by their intense religious life and heroic enthusiasm. Since, in these early ages they lived with their own families, their virtuous mode of living was well known to all the people. Already in this second century a hymn of virginal chastity resounds from every corner of Christ's kingdom. Virgins are found not merely in certain isolated places, but in the entire Church: in Egypt, in Palestine, in Syria, in Asia Minor, in Greece, in North Africa, in Rome.

From the middle of the second century practically all priests were celibates. This seems to have inspired many lay people to live virginal lives. Perhaps some of the women sought in virginity a substitute for the fact that they could not be priests. Their lives of perfect chastity were an offering of incense most pleasing to God. They continued to live with their familes and enjoyed a normal social life, except that they avoided the public baths, which were often immoral, and wedding banquets. They engaged in the apostolate of charity, but their specific type of work is unknown. They were not afraid of martyrdom, because through martyrdom their goal was attained more easily and perfectly. Many of them from now on were called on to shed their blood in testimony of their purity as well as faith. Out of the second century the Church honors these Saints: St. Balbina (Mar. 31), St. Blandina (June 2), St. Praxedes (July 21), St. Pudentiana (May 19), St. Serapia (July 29).

The Greek physician and medical writer, Claudius Galenus, of the second century, gives this nice testimony:

[The Christians] observe a conduct worthy of true philosophers. The fact that they despise death is right before our eyes; likewise, that, guided by modesty, they abstain from the use of sex. In fact, there are among them both men and women who during their entire life abstain from sexual intercourse.[89]

The purity of the early Christians, especially of the virgins, which was such a contrast to what the pagan world had known, was really a moral miracle. It would not have been possible without the special intervention of God. Christ had espoused His Virgin Church to Himself on the cross amid crucifying pains. Then it was that He imparted to His Church His spirit of sacrifice and courage, even in the face of death, to live a life of purity. Virgin souls are the living monuments to this spirit. If it is true in general, and it is, that the blood of the martyrs is the seed of Christians, then it was quite true that the blood of the virgin martyrs was **the seed of many, many more virgins.**

With the beginning of the third century—Tertullian is our witness—virgins began to take vows. Or, perhaps better stated, then we have the first recorded testimony of the fact, which seems to have been older in practice. With the end of the third century and the beginning of the fourth the virgins began slowly to retire into the solitude of the deserts and to live in communities. The third century is rich with names of well-known virgin Saints: Agatha (Feb. 5), Agnes of Rome (Jan. 21), Apollonia (Feb. 9), Cecilia (Nov. 22), Emerentiana (Jan. 23), Justina of Antioch (Sept. 26), Margaret (July 20), Martina (Jan. 30), Rufina and Secunda (July 10), Susanna (Aug. 11).

During the fourth century the ecclesiastical institution of virginity reached its height. A distinction was made between those who merely made a promise to live in chastity and those who were consecrated by a public ceremony. Before such a consecration there was a time of probation for the virgin. In Rome the age required for the consecration was twenty-five. At other places it was often much higher, even forty years. The ceremonial was still rather simple. There was an address by the Bishop, the profession or renewal of vow, the giving of the veil and the blessing. The names were placed in a church record. The virgins were reminded of Christ's promise of a hundredfold reward.

Various effects followed such a consecration. The virgins were given a place of honor in church assemblies, near the deaconesses and widows, who followed the priests and deacons. Seduction of such a virgin was regarded a great crime, punished by the Church and God. If the virgin sinned deliberately against the vow, she was classed as a penitent and obliged to do severe penances. The virgins were given particular rules of life to remain loyal to their calling. They were to practice mortifications and observe fasts and abstain from meat and wine. They were not to attend banquets and public baths. The hairdo was to be very simple. Their clothes were to be of a dark color and modest style. The virgins were encouraged to give alms and to pray the Psalter and read the Scriptures. They were to keep themselves busy, since idleness is dangerous to purity. Many of them took part in ecclesiastical processions and sang hymns. They also helped at baptisms. Most of them still lived with their families.

Out of the fourth century we have such Saints as Barbara (Dec. 4), Bibiana (Dec. 2), Catherine of Alexandria (Nov. 25), Dorothy (Feb. 6), Eulalia of Barcelona (Feb. 12) and Eulalia of Merida (Dec. 10), Euphemia (Sept. 16), Justina of Padua (Oct. 7), Lucy (Dec. 13), Macrina the Younger (July 19). These are only a small number of the thousands who lived a virginal life. Parents hid their daughters from St. Ambrose, lest he persuade them to become virgins. Pope Liberius himself consecrated St. Ambrose's sister, Marcellina, in St. Peter's Basilica. St. Irene, the sister of Pope St. Damasus, had herself enrolled among the choirs of virgins. St. Helena, mother of Emperor Constantine, when practically eighty years old, visited at Jerusalem. Before leaving she wished to pay special honor to the virgins there. She called all together for a banquet and herself served them. All in all, virginal life was enjoying great honor in the Church.

In the fifth century St. Augustine, no doubt by hyperbole, tells us that there were more virgins than married women. But at that time a great change was taking place. Virgins generally lived a common life in convents, which some of them founded. Soon such outnumbered those that lived alone in the world. The ceremonial for consecration, too, became more elaborate. Its prayers stressed the ideals of virginity and petitioned for the grace of loyalty. About this time the Empress Pulcheria of Constantinople (d. 453) helped much to spread esteem for virginal life. So did St. Genevieve (d. 512), the patroness of Paris.

Matters progressed rather evenly from then until the tenth century. From the tenth century till the twelfth there were two different rites of consecration: one for the nuns in convents, and one for the virgins in the world. The giving of the ring and the wreath was added to the ceremony at this time.

During the feudal ages many of the daughters of the feudal princes lived a virginal life, at times under greatest hardships. Of this era we can meniton St. Zita of Italy (d. 1278), patroness of domestic workers, St. Notburga of Tyrol (d. 1313), St. Rose of Viterbo, Franciscan Tertiary (d. 1252), and St. Catherine of Siena, Dominican Tertiary (d. 1380).

That virginal life was still held in high esteem during the Middle Ages is evidenced by the literature of the times. Later, however, under Humanism, which stressed the cult of the body too much, the atmosphere was not so favorable for virginal life. After the sixteenth century the consecration of virgins was rare in convents as well as in the world. Even St. Charles Borromeo was reluctant to renew the ceremony in convents. Still virginal life was lived even in the world during this epoch, in spite of the many difficulties, as is shown by the work of Herman Busenbaum, S.J., *Lilies among the Thorns*, written in 1660. Examples of sainted and saintly virgins of these centuries are: Catherine of Cordona, Italy (d. 1577), St. Germaine Cousin of Toulouse (d. 1601), St. Rose of Lima, Peru (d. 1617), St. Marianna Paredes of Jesus, the Lily of Quito (d. 1645), Armella of Brittany (d. 1671), Helen Priscopi of Padua (d. 1684), Agnes Pfeiffer of Finthen near Mainz (d. 1754), Mary Eustella of Saintes, France (d. 1842). Of special interest to us Americans is the Venerable Kateri Tekakwitha, the Lily of the Mohawks, whose cause for beatification is progressing nicely. When she was twenty-three she made a vow of perpetual virginity, which a year later she crowned by martyrdom.

A new era for virginal living seems to have begun in the middle of the nineteenth century, after the definition of the Immaculate Conception. Mary, under that title, became the special patroness of virgins. It was then too that a noteworthy increase in literature on virginal living began to appear. The great liturgist, Dom Guéranger, did much for restoring the consecration ceremony for virgins in convents. In recent years the Holy See has permitted this ceremony in some convents. As late as March 25, 1927, however, she forbade it for people in the world.[90] And still there is a movement on foot, especially in France, to allow the ceremony even for people in the world, as an incentive for living this ideal of Christianity.

Since the end of World War II the movement for recognition of the vocation of single men and women living in virginity in the world has increased by leaps and bounds. The canonization of St. Mary Goretti, a martyr to chastity in the world, has helped not a little to promote this movement. On the other hand, the deaths of many young men in the armies of Catholic countries of Europe left many a woman without an opportunity for marriage. These women had to resign themselves to the single life of chastity. Divine Providence often works through natural causes. God may have used this calamity of the war to recall to Christians the dignity of the single vocation of perfect chastity lived in the world. One might be able to call this present era the second spring of the modern interest in the Christian ideal of virginal life in the world.

Men who wish to live this life have been given an outstanding model in Blessed Contardo Ferrini, who lived in our own day. He made a private vow of chastity and lived as a layman, since he did not feel himself called to the priesthood or religious life. He practiced not only heroic virtue, but accomplished much in the field of Catholic Action through his teaching and scholarly works. We must mention also the virgin of Lucca, St. Gemma Galgani, who because of ill-health could not be a religious. She lived a life of perfect virginity amid intense sufferings. Today we are beginning to hear much of the late Edel Quinn, the young lady who was too feeble to be a Poor Clare Nun, but who did heroic work as envoy of the Legion of Mary for seven years in African mission fields.

Many others there are, men and women, who have gone to their eternal reward in the recent past, or who are still laboring in the Lord's vineyard, who dedicated their chastity to the Divine Spouse and their charity to His Virgin Bride and their Mother, the Church. The Book of Life lists their names in letters of gold. Time may bring a number of them more prominently into the limelight of the Church. Each and every one of these heroic brides of Christ are shining examples for imitation.

CHAPTER THIRTEEN

Chastity and Modesty

SINCE THE PRACTICE OF CHASTITY IS THE CHARACTERISTIC virtue of those who consecrate their single lives to Christ, we shall discuss the safeguarding and perfecting of chastity. It hardly needs proof that virginal and perfect chastity must be safeguarded and perfected. It would never do to choose this form of life and then be careless or indifferent about committing sins against chastity. Those who pledge themselves to live in perfect chastity must always keep their lamps trimmed in readiness for the coming of the Bridegroom (cf. Matthew 25,1). They must give Christ the undivided love that they promised.

The practice of chastity has both a negative and a positive aspect. The negative aspect is that of striving to overcome all temptations against purity and of never offending Christ by sins of impurity or immodesty. The positive aspect is that of loving Christ always more perfectly and all other creatures in, through, and for Christ.

A fundamental principle for safeguarding purity is to know precisely what purity is and what are sins against it. This, of course, not for the purpose of knowing how far one can go without sinning, but for the purpose of having a correct and balanced notion about when one is pure, for peace of conscience in fighting against temptations, and for striving for the highest purity with calm intelligence.

It is necessary, then, that we study both the virtue and the sins against purity. Some there are who think that once they have determined to live a chaste life, especially after they have had some success in avoiding sins, they can forget about mortal sins against chastity and concentrate merely on the higher motives of virginal love for Christ. True, as one becomes more perfect these higher motives should come to the fore and be more influential; but as long as one is living in this world one will never attain a degree of perfection in chastity so high that one will be exempt from keeping in mind what precisely is sinful in thought, desire, and deed. In fact, the remembrance of the possibility of committing these sins helps very much to be victorious over temptations.

Chastity may be defined as the natural and supernatural habit that regulates, according to right reason and faith, the sentient appetite in the use of the sex powers and in the enjoyment of the sexual pleasures. Since this is a virtuous habit, it must be internal. Though chastity deals with the physical organs and powers of sex, it is in its innermost nature not physical but spiritual, moral. It is a matter of the mind, of the intellect and will; it is essentially internal.

Our broad definition, about regulating the use and pleasure of sex, includes the purity of the married as well as of the single; it fits the complete continence of the single who are still waiting for an opportunity of marriage as well as those who have chosen the single life as their vocation.

Purity is the rational control of the use of sex according to God's laws. It is not insensibility to the sexual emotions; it is not sexual coldness. In fact, a person who is sexually frigid could be interiorly very immoral. Neither, then, is sexual coldness or a passionless nature the goal toward which purity strives. Real purity does not try to make people insensible to the sex passion, much less does it attempt to eradicate the sexual power. It tries to control sex, to keep it within the bounds of divine law. For the single that means to abstain completely from all use of sex and from the enjoyment of sex pleasure.

We have in mind here not merely the natural virtue of chastity, which would be guided only by reason, and could exist in a pagan. We have in mind also the supernatural virtue, which is supported by grace and guided by faith, by the revealed laws of God. Divine revelation has opened vistas upon purity that were but faintly, if at all, visible before. Especially has it put in clear light the possibility and excellence of perpetual renunciation of the privileges of married life and of sex pleasure, namely, of virginal chastity.

Virginity or virginal chastity is the firm resolve of one who has never voluntarily lost carnal integrity to abstain perpetually from all sexual pleasure, not only the illicit but also the licit pleasure in married life. Two elements belong to the essence of virginity: carnal integrity and the firm resolve of perpetual perfect chastity. Let us note that the resolve of virginity may be strengthened by a vow, but that is not necessary.

Carnal integrity is had when one has never *voluntarily* induced, or consented to, *complete* sexual pleasure, whether in copulation or in solitary act. This essential element for carnal integrity is the same for male and female. In the female the orifice of the vagina is partially closed by a membrane called the hymen. Normally this is broken by the first copulation. The unbroken hymen is, therefore, normally an external sign of carnal integrity in a female. But not always, because the hymen may be broken by other actions, such as horseback riding; and because in some females the hymen is so lax that it is merely enlarged, not broken, by copulation. Hence the broken hymen is a sign of the loss of virginity only when it was broken by the *voluntary* action of copulation, or by some other *voluntary* action for the sake of sex pleasure. But because normally the physical phenomenon of an unbroken hymen obtains only in the female, it is from her the terms "virgin" and "virginity," take their native and physiological meaning, though by derivation and morally they are used of the male as well, because the moral element and the essence of carnal integrity is the same for male and female: the absence of any voluntary enjoyment of complete sexual pleasure.

Virginity can, therefore, be lost in the following manner. This consideration will help to clarify the nature of virginity. Virginity is not lost by the loss of mere carnal integrity without any voluntary consent to that loss. And so it is not lost by involuntary pollution, as during sleep, or by involuntary, forced copulation, as in rape. In this last case, the woman's organ is no longer physically intact, that is, the external sign of virginity is no longer there, but before God she is still a virgin. Virginity in both the carnal and moral sense is lost by a *voluntary* consent to *complete* sexual pleasure; that is, by voluntary pollution or by copulation, in either man or woman. This pollution will always be a mortal sin. The copulation will be no sin at all if had with the lawful marriage partner and if there was no vow of virginity. It is self-evident that once carnal-moral virginity is lost, namely, by voluntary complete sexual pleasure, it is lost for all time; it can never be repaired.

Virginity in the moral sense alone (namely, without loss of carnal integrity) may be lost in two ways. First, by the intention (quite legitimate in one who has no vow of virginity) of marrying and of consummating the marriage. It is, therefore, not lost by the mere intention of marrying if one does not intend to consummate the marriage by making use of the rights of marriage. Secondly, it is lost by any and every *internal* mortal sin against chastity, and by any voluntary consent to incomplete sexual pleasure. Complete sexual pleasure does not enter here, because by it also carnal integrity is lost. If one loses virginity only in this moral sense, it can be repaired. First, if it was lost by the intention of marrying and of making use of the marriage rights, it can be repaired by the revocation of that intention before the marriage is actually consummated, and by the renewal of the resolve to live in perpetual chastity. Secondly, if it was lost by a mortal sin against chastity, which did not violate carnal integrity, it can be repaired by contrition and penance.

Modesty is very closely connected with chastity. Really it exists only because of chastity. It controls all acts that might, indirectly, arouse the sex passion in oneself or in others. Modesty is, therefore, the protection of chastity. Though modesty is essentially an internal act of the will, it is expressed also in external actions. These may be grouped under four heads: sight, touch, speech, reading.

Modesty of sight is twofold: modesty in looking at objects and modesty in appearance, namely, in presenting oneself to the looks of others. Modesty in looking means to guard the eyes against looking at objects that would arouse the sex appetite to commit sins of impurity. Modesty in appearance demands the reasonable covering of such members of the body as would, when exposed, be a stimulant to sex in oneself or in others. Modesty in appearance demands, too, that one avoid in posture, gait, or gestures, in particular in dancing and in theatrical performances, whatever may be a stimulant to sex in normal people. Modesty demands that men avoid all that is effeminate or suggestive in their behavior, and that women avoid all that is bold and masculine. Modesty of touch commands that one abstain from all unnecessary touching of objects that would result in arousing the sex passion in normal people. Modesty of speech, including song, means avoiding all words that might arouse the sex passion. This includes all suggestive and double-meaning words, jokes and stories, as well as such that are directly and expressly about sex matters. Modesty in reading avoids reading that will incite sexual pleasure. Besides these four groups of modest actions, we can practice modesty in thought by not thinking about sex matters or sins, without good reason, if such thinking starts the imagination to work and thus incites to passion.

Modesty is a moral virtue and as such it must strive for the golden mean, neither swerving too far to the left nor to the right. It must avoid pruriency as well as prudishness. Pruriency is a curiosity for matters that indirectly touch sex. Prudishness is an excessive reserve and fear of being immodest where there need be no fear.

To be able to observe the virtue of chastity more calmly and wisely and to strive for purity with a well-balanced attitude because of a clear knowledge of what is sinful and what is not, it is of great help to have correct ideas about the physiology and psychology of sex. By itself, of course, such knowledge is not a guarantee against sin, but neither is ignorance of those things a criterion of purity. Since, however, I judged the description of these matters outside the scope of my work, I refer the readers who may need and desire such information to the inexpensive but excellent booklet of Father Gerald Kelly, S.J., *Modern Youth and Chastity*.[91]

One cannot strive for purity prudently without a clear knowledge of what is impure and what immodest. But, again, we suppose this knowledge in those who are thinking about dedicating themselves to perfect purity. For those who need information on these matters, Father Kelly's booklet should prove adequate. Since, however, the control of one's mind in these matters is of utmost importance, I shall give a review of the internal sins of impurity and immodesty.

All interior sins against chastity and modesty are popularly often referred to as impure thoughts. There are, however, three distinct interior sins of impurity and one of immodesty: the impure desire, the impure delight, the impure thought, the immodest thought.

An impure desire is the sin of deliberately desiring to commit a sin of impurity. The object of the desire is a *future* act. But the sin of desire is committed when the desire is elicited, even if one actually never carries out the desire. The sinful desire has the same malice as the sin one desires to commit. If the sin desired is that of pollution, so is the desire, and so on. It is well known that Christ insisted against the Pharisees that such a desire of adultery is already the sin of adultery (cf. Matthew 5,27-28).

Impure delight is of two kinds, according as the object of the delight is a past sin or a present imagined sinful sex action. First, an impure delight is the sin of rejoicing over a sin of impurity that has been committed by oneself or another. The object of such a delight is a *past* sin. This impure delight has the same sinfulness as the past sin over which one delights. Such rejoicing is, namely, a consent to and approval of the sin. It is, therefore, to be judged by the rules for direct sins of impurity: If the past sin was mortal, the delight is mortal; if the past sin was fornication, so is the delight in it. Secondly, an impure delight is the intentional and wilful approval of and delight in some specific impure action that one is thinking of, and which one may be representing in the imagination, but which one does not desire to commit in deed. Usually this is called the sin of morose delectation. There is here a *direct* will to think about sex actions, or if they have arisen involuntarily, to continue to think about them, with the set purpose of mentally rejoicing in the sex action. The sexual pleasure enjoyed mentally is willed directly, so this is not just an immodest thought, as in the next group to be discussed.

The sin of impure delight is committed even if there is actually no sexual pleasure aroused in the sentient appetite, or before that is aroused. If over and above this inner sin of impure delight sexual pleasure is aroused, this must be judged by the regular rules of any sexual pleasure. If consent is given to it, there is also an external sin of impurity. If consent is denied, then at least this external sin was not committed.

To think about matters pertaining to sex, even about sins of impurity, for some direct purpose that is lawful can, nevertheless, be stimulating to passion. So one must apply the principles of an indirect voluntary action: there must be a good reason for positing the thinking about sex matters, a good reason that is proportionate in gravity to the danger of stimulating passion and the liability of consent. One may never think about such matters directly for the intention of stimulating sex. To do so would be a direct sin of impurity by intention.

When there is a proximate liability of giving consent to the sex pleasure that may be aroused by such thinking, one may think about the sex matters only if one has a real necessity for doing so, and even then one must make every effort to reduce the proximate liability to a remote one by applying the rules for resisting temptations.

If such thoughts are strongly stimulating to passion and create a *proximate* danger to *complete* sex pleasure, one must have a grave reason for licitly engaging in them. Such a grave reason is had by those who must study such matters for their profession (doctors, lawyers, priests, and so on), or for their vocation (couples about to marry). So if one has such a grave reason, he commits no sin of immodesty by such thoughts, even if he foresees that pollution will result, and actually does, provided he gives no consent to this. If one has a good reason, but one that is not sufficiently grave, according to reliable authors one commits only a venial sin by engaging in thoughts that might result in sexual pleasure. If one has no good reason at all, one commits a mortal sin. If one were to engage in such thoughts out of levity and curiosity, in which case they would be only *remotely* stimulating, there would be only a venial sin. If the thoughts are such that by their nature they are only remotely stimulating to complete sexual pleasure, though proximately to incomplete pleasure, barring an impure intention and proximate liability to consent, one would commit only a venial sin by such thoughts if there is no good reason for them; and no sin at all, if there is some good reason for them.

If such thoughts about sex matters and sex sins arise involuntarily, one must judge their morality by what happens after one becomes aware of their presence. Often thoughts are in the mind unconsciously and one might continue to daydream about them a while before really being conscious of their presence as stimulating to passion. In that case, one measures the morality only from one's reaction to them after one becomes aware of them. This principle will save one from many a useless worry about impure thoughts or immodest thoughts that one has seemingly been guilty of, but actually not.

It goes without saying that one should rid his mind of

thoughts that stimulate passion as soon as he is aware of them and has no sufficient reason for continuing them. This policy of prompt rejection of impure and immodest thoughts is one of the best safeguards against sins of impurity and immodesty.

If thoughts persist in the mind, especially when they are also focussed on the imagination, there is no sin so long as one does not wish to have them and tries to rid himself of them and shows disapproval of them in some manner. As long as that is done, there is no sin but great virtue. Sometimes people are worried about having committed sin because of mere temptations, when in reality they practiced a high degree of virtue. Calmness in persistent impure thoughts is a great asset to victory. But one should learn to hate whatever really offends modesty and shun it always.

Since a person who desires to live a life of perfect chastity and forego marriage may seal that resolve by a vow, it is well to note how he might sin by desiring marriage or actually entering marriage. Only if a person has made a vow, that is, freely bound himself under the added virtue of religion to live a single life of perfect chastity would he commit a sin against religion by desiring to get married and actually marrying. But since one could get a dispensation from such a vow, one could desire to marry on condition that one will get dispensed. We spoke earlier about such dispensations. To marry without a dispensation would be a sin, but the marriage would be valid (Canon Law, n. 1058, 1). A person who has made a vow, even though only private, cannot dispense himself. He must be dispensed by a priest who has the proper faculty.

If one has vowed to live in perfect chastity or virginity, any violation of chastity will also be a sin against religion. If one has vowed chastity under pain of venial sin, then a violation of chastity will be a venial sin against religion, plus a mortal or venial sin against chastity. If one has vowed to observe chastity under mortal sin, then any violation of chastity that is a mortal sin would also be a mortal sin against religion, and any violation of chastity that is only a venial sin, would be only a venial sin against religion.

Chapter Fourteen

Some Basic Helps in Safeguarding Purity

IN ORDER TO SAFEGUARD AND PERFECT ANY GIVEN VIRTUE it is necessary to strive for improvement in every virtue. That holds equally for the virtue of chastity, as the Churchmen inculcated in their writings. It would, then, be worthwhile to pursue an entire course in the spiritual life, in order to live a well-balanced and successful single life of perfect chastity in the world. Such a complete course is beyond the scope of the present work. I wish, however, to offer brief descriptions of some basic helps for remaining chaste and for perfecting the lily of the virtues.

The promise, even under vow, to live a single life of perfect chastity is no guarantee of freedom from temptations to impurity. Indeed, the very fact of having made a vow renouncing all sexual pleasure makes it psychologically possible and probable that the temptations to enjoy sexual pleasure will on occasion be even more bothersome. One continues to have the passion of sex in spite of the vow; one cannot discard it as one can discard wealth by a vow of poverty. So let there be no mistake: there will be temptations.

One should, therefore, not be surprised or depressed if

at any time one has to endure temptations, perhaps a longer siege. A single person is never too young or too old in such a life that he may not have temptations. He is never so perfect that there may not be severe trials against purity. There may be special trials in the earlier period of such a single life, with comparative freedom from temptations later. One may be spared in the earlier years, on the other hand, only to endure grave temptations later. There is no particular pattern according to which the devil will tempt a person in this matter; nor is there a uniform plan according to which God permits such tests of virtue. That makes little difference. What matters is that one is always on the alert for an offensive against temptations whenever and wherever they may appear, and that one builds up a strong defensive against any surprise attack. Such vigilance is an important tactic in the fight against temptations. Our Holy Father places it first in his list of means for persevering in purity (*On Holy Virginity*, p. 182), and he mentions it several other times (pp. 180, 182 f.). It is precisely the struggle that one must put up in defense of purity that makes the difficult commandment a continuous sacrifice, even a living martyrdom (cf. *On Holy Virginity*, p. 180).

It might be well to note here that some people are of a colder nature in regard to sex than others. They are not bothered much with sexual passion. That does not, of itself, indicate that they are more chaste than those who might be more sensitive to sexual passion. In fact, one who is of a more affectionate nature can, by the greater fight it takes to remain pure, merit a richer supply of grace and more satisfying heavenly happiness. This opportunity of greater merit and more solid virtue, because of the greater struggle of more affectionate persons, was dramatically emphasized already by St. Methodius in the conclusion to his *The Banquet of the Ten Virgins*, Discourse 11, Ch. 3.[92]

Such a more affectionate nature, furthermore, can be a greater help in loving Christ more ardently and intensely. The same heart in Mary Magdalene that first squandered itself in lust later surrendered itself most generously in love toward the Sacred Heart of Jesus. The more ardent and affectionate one's nature for being an ideal spouse and parent, so much more is one fit to be a perfect bride of Christ.

Grace, God's supernatural help, is the indispensable means for avoiding sins of impurity. It is all-sufficient for victory. How consoling is not God's answer to St. Paul. The Apostle was enduring a very severe trial, the nature of which is not certain. Three times he had begged for relief. Then came the answer from God: "My grace is sufficient for you, for strength is made perfect in weakness" (2 Corinthians, 12,9). God's grace will make the difficult virtue a realized fruit of the Holy Spirit. His gift is never wanting. What Paul says of temptations in general is quite true for trials of purity:

Therefore, let him who thinks he stands take heed lest he fall. May no temptation take hold of you but such as man is equal to. God is faithful and will not permit you to be tempted beyond your strength, but with the temptation will also give you a way out that you may be able to bear it. (1 Corinthians 10,13)

Because of the need of grace for victory, and because God ordinarily awaits our request for grace, it is imperative that we pray for victory when temptations assail us. There are some natural psychological tactics for diverting the mind from evil suggestions that have their value; but prayer, if intelligently used, will always be *the* psychological weapon against temptations, because it diverts the mind's attention into higher spheres of value. Our Holy Father notes with St. Alphonsus Liguori "that there is no help more necessary and certain for conquering temptations against the beautiful virtue of chastity than instant recourse to God in prayer" [93] (*On Holy Virginity*, p. 187). Christ will not allow His bride to fall into sin if she has recourse to Him in time of need.

But prayer as a means of preserving and perfecting purity may not be confined to a cry for help in actual temptation. One must petition God frequently, daily, for the grace of perseverance in this virtue. That is the advice of the Pope (*On Holy Virginity*, p. 182, 187). He is but echoing the wisdom of the saints, as he notes,[94] and even of Christ, whose admonition to watch and pray, lest one fall into temptation (Matthew 26,41), was never more needed than for purity.

Yet more, the scope of prayer in reference to purity may not be confined to petitioning grace. One must take a general interest in developing a spirit of prayer: an absorbing interest in wishing to converse with one's Spouse at every opportunity. Was it not greater freedom to devote more time and energy to prayer that made one choose this vocation of perfect chastity? Is that not the essential purpose for living this life? We must, then, indulge in prayer to our heart's content, and it will become a powerful means of remaining pure and of perfecting the positive element in consecrated purity, love of Christ.

In prayer, then, the pure bride of Christ must find her delight. Even in mental prayer she must learn to acquire a more profound understanding of the mysteries of God, especially of the mystery of God's love for her. In mental prayer she must learn to enjoy the closest friendship with her Spouse.

There should, therefore, be a planned program of prayer,

of spiritual exercises, for each week and each day. It should not be too cumbersome so it will be observed. It should not be so full that it is more fatiguing than helpful. It should be flexible enough that one can adjust it to unforeseen events and circumstances. There should be a time for the Holy Sacrifice of the Mass and for Communion, each day if possible. There should be a period of mental prayer, at least fifteen minutes a day. This should be preferably part of the morning prayer. If that is not possible, it can be made any time later when suitable. Besides, there should be definite vocal morning prayers and evening prayers, short, concise and to the point. The daily Rosary should find a place in the life of a single person. Occasional visits to the Blessed Sacrament should be planned, if possible. A regular period of spiritual reading should be fit into the daily program, or at least into the weekly program. The single person in love with Christ will avail himself of the opportunities of monthly recollections and annual retreat.

As a very special aid in this matter of prayer for purity one must note devotion to the Holy Spirit, the Spirit of Divine Love. Grace, according to the beautiful idea of St. Paul, makes a human person a temple of the Holy Spirit (1 Corinthians 6,19). His seven special Gifts—in fact He Himself—are the peculiar dowry that the Bridegroom Christ gives to the virgin soul. And among His fruits continence holds a place of honor (cf. Galatians 5,23).

It is the Holy Spirit who guards His own temple inviolate. It was He who made the perpetual virginity of Mary a possibility and a reality, even while she became the Mother of God. It was He who protected St. Lucy miraculously against those who wished to violate her virginity. It is the Holy Spirit, then, who is in a special way the Divine Advocate as well as Consoler of virgin souls.

It is easy, too, to pray to Him who is so near to Christ's virgin brides, who dwells so intimately in the souls through His grace and gifts. Call often on this most intimate Friend of yours; live always conscious of His consoling and protective Presence.

In fighting actual temptations, to retreat from the occasion of the temptation is very chivalrous and courageous. One must have a genuine distrust of self and a fear of offending God. And because of that one must flee from the occasions of the temptations as much as possible. One cannot court danger in this respect and expect to remain pure. The Book of Proverbs asks rhetorically:

> Can a man take fire to his bosom,
> And his garments not be burned? (6,27).

On this score the Holy Father remarked:

In regard to that point, further, We must call attention—a matter taught by the Holy Fathers[95] and the Doctors of the Church[96]—that we can more easily fight against and restrain the enticements of sin and the allurements of the passions if we do not struggle against them directly, but rather flee from them as best we can. To safeguard chastity, according to Jerome's teaching, flight is more effective than open battle: "I flee precisely that I may not be overcome." [97] (*On Holy Virginity*, p. 183)

The Pope explains what is meant by such flight:

Such flight must be understood in the sense that we not only diligently avoid the occasion of sin, but especially that in such battles we elevate the mind and heart to divine things, being chiefly intent on Him to whom we have vowed our virginity. "Gaze on the beauty of your lover," is the advice St. Augustine gives.[98] (*On Holy Virginity*, p. 183)

After that the Pope refutes in two more paragraphs the insidious error of those moderns who think that people dedicated to chastity, priests in particular, should take risks and put chastity to the test, especially by contact with the world. The Pope begins his remarks with this statement:

Now, such flight and constant vigilance, by which we must diligently keep far from us occasions of sin, were considered in every age by holy men and women as the most fit method in this kind of warfare. (*On Holy Virginity*, p. 183)

To that we should like to add: One who has promised to live a single life of chastity must avoid not only the usual occasions of impurity but also all things that, though quite lawful for the marriageable, might endanger the vocation of the single life of perfect chastity.

To the tactics of flight we can attach also the tactic of retreating mentally from a temptation by substituting an absorbing thought in place of an impure or immodest suggestion. One cannot drive a temptation away as one might drive away a mad dog with a stick, or throw it out, as one might throw a burning rug out a window. But one can substitute other thoughts in place of sinful suggestions. It is most profitable to train oneself to make such substitution of thought quickly. One class of thoughts that can absorb one's attention in an instant is thoughts about accidents, perhaps the recollection of a very close call from one's own experience.

Though one should be constantly on the alert against temptations, one should not be on the alert *for* temptations. In other words, the fear that one should have of offending God by impurity should not be an undue fear of temptations, a fear that would like to be entirely free from temptations of the flesh, and would consider perhaps even temptations to be sins. The more one fears temptations, in the wrong sense, the more temptations one will have. If a man walks through a dark place afraid of ghosts, he will see ghosts everywhere. If one is over-anxious about temptations against the flesh, they will be impressed still more and multiplied. Have no unholy fear of temptations; they are not sins. Know the difference between temptation and sin. Fear falling into sin.

Self-denial, according to all masters of the spiritual life, is essential for preserving chastity. Chastity must live on a spirit of sacrifice, just as it was born of a spirit of sacrifice. The bare renunciation of sinful pleasure is not enough. One must aim at a high ideal of self-denial even in matters that are otherwise lawful. Spiritual writers cannot impress these points too deeply on the soul. That is why the saints were so severe with themselves for preserving purity. To treat the body and its senses with indulgence, to deny it no satisfaction, and then to expect to keep the sex passion under control is utter folly. As might be expected, our Holy Father stresses the need of self-denial.

For that reason we must, in the first place, be watchful over the movements of the passions and the senses, and so check them even by voluntary severity and bodily chastisement, that we might make them submissive to right reason and God's law. . . . All holy men and women carefully watched over the movements of their senses and passions, and at times sharply restrained them, in keeping with the words of the Divine Master Himself who taught: "But I say to you that anyone who even looks with lust at a woman has already committed adultery with her in his heart. So if your right eye is an occasion of sin to you, pluck it out and cast it from you; it is better for you that one of your members should perish than that your whole body should be thrown into hell" (Matthew 5,28-29). By this admonition, as is very clear, our Redeemer demands of us, first, that we do not give in to sin even mentally, and that with firm determination we keep far from us everything that can sully this most beautiful virtue even in the slightest manner. In this matter no diligence can be thought too great, no severity too great. If ill-health or other causes do not permit an individual the more severe bodily austerities, still these never exempt such a one from vigilance and the inner self-control. (*On Holy Virginity*, p. 182)

This need of self-control is most imperative today for one who lives in the world, because the world is a constant temptation to live a sensuous life, and even to allow sex to dominate everything. The modern world regards man chiefly as a sexual being. Sex is the center of everything. Sex must enter into sports, into the arts, into recreation, into literature, into drama, into movies, into television—into everything. To practice perfect chastity in such a world, there is need of a spirit of self-denial.

Moreover, the very fact that one has renounced all sex pleasure may incline his passions to seek a substitute in sensual pleasure, in a confortable home, in recreation of all sorts. There must, then, be a daily development of a spirit of self-denial in. regard to bodily pleasures, in regard to the senses of sight, hearing, touch, taste, in regard to reading, friendships, and idleness. But it must be a spirit of self-denial, that is, an inner interest in, and readiness for, denying oneself out of love for purity, not merely an external mortification. That spirit will suggest acts of self-denial compatible with one's health, and will not urge the omission of all self-denial on grounds of ill-health.

There must be mortifications of the body as well as of

the senses and of the mind. Mortifications of the higher faculties of the intellect and will are not enough. One must do some mortifying of the body as well. And this can be done even by those who may be ill. Their mortifying of the body will not be the same as that of a healthy person, but mortification of the body it will be.

One of the best means of self-denial for preserving chastity, for controlling of the sex appetite, is the control of the appetite for food and drink. A fundamental rule in regard to food and drink for one who desires to live chastely and perfect this virtue always more is: Moderation always! That constant observance of moderation in food and drink will be a splendid means for building a spirit of self-denial and a most effective weapon against temptations. Moreover, one can always find special occasions for mortifying one's taste by eating without complaint food that is not prepared according to the best rules of the culinary art, or by being satisfied with less when an insufficient quantity has been prepared. One can find many an occasion of mortification by passing up food that is very tasty but that has little nourishing value.

The law of moderation will, of course, always be observed in regard to alcoholic drinks. In fact, if total abstinence is in place for any Christian, it is certainly so for one who has consecrated to Christ the complete renunciation of sex pleasure. Abstinence from alcoholic drinks is an excellent companion to abstinence from sex pleasure. Not that one should abstain from strong liquor because of an erroneous view that that is of strict obligation for everyone, or that one cannot drink it at any time in any quantity without sinning. Not at all! One should abstain from it freely for the higher purpose of safeguarding and perfecting chastity ever more out of love for Christ. The same motivation, in other words, that was at work for completely renouncing sex pleasure itself should be at work in renouncing the pleasure of taste.

Mortification of the senses is paramount. This should be self-evident from the fact that sexual pleasure is stimulated by the indirect actions of the senses. The Church writers insisted on the need of mortifying the senses. St. Methodius referred to the five senses as the five pathways of virtue that must be kept pure for Christ; and he compared the body to a five-light lamp, which the soul will carry on meeting the Bridegroom on the day of the resurrection.[99] This doctrine of the need of mortifying the senses is contained, too, in the teaching of the Fathers about the need of modesty. On this St. Ambrose writes:

> Everywhere in the Virgin [Mary] modesty is the companion of her singular virtues. This must be the inseparable companion of virginity, without which virginity cannot exist.[100]

As for mortification of the imagination and of the intellect and will, one who is interested in a spirit of self-denial will find many an occasion. I should like to mention a few special points of self-denial. Those who are striving for greater perfection by perfect chastity can easily become too critical of others who have not so bound themselves. They should curb such criticism. Again, some may demonstrate too much curiosity about the status of the married and marriageable in their neighborhood. An excellent field of inner self-denial. Some may become kind of exhibitionists of their "greater" perfection. Humility is a splendid form of self-denial and a superb means of preserving purity.

Finally, an unparalleled instrument of self-denial and penance is the sacrament of Confession, in which one must unveil his inner self in its ugliest form. In the narrow confessional there is no room for swell-headed pride. Besides, there is no humanly invented psychological tactic for fighting temptations that can equal, much less surpass, the divine sacrament of Confession. Regular and sincere confession is the best means for keeping the Devil of impurity at a respectable distance. He despises the sincere and regular baring of one's smallest faults with a view to guarding against any laxness that may lead to bigger sins.

In Chapter Ten we spoke at length about the relation of the Virgin Mother of Jesus to the vocation of virginity. Here, as a means for safeguarding and perfecting purity, we wish to say a few words about devotion to the Blessed Mother under two heads: Model and Mediatrix. Of this the Pope wrote:

A solid and very fervent devotion toward God's Virgin Mother is certainly an eminent means, as has been tested by experience over and over again through the centuries. By it chastity is preserved and cherished unblemished and perfect. In a sense all other aids are contained in this devotion: because whoever is sincerely and earnestly animated by it will undoubtedly be salutarily stirred up to be constantly vigilant, to pour forth prayers, and to approach the Tribunal of Penance and the Holy Table. On that acount We give the paternal exhortation to all priests and religious men and holy virgins that they have recourse to the special protection of God's loving Mother, who is the Virgin of virgins and "the teacher of virginity," [101] as Ambrose assures us, and who is the most powerful Mother especially of all who dedicate and consecrate themselves to the divine service. (*On Holy Virginity*, p. 187 f.)

Mary is, next to Jesus, the peerless model of perfect purity and consecrated virginity. The Holy Father ends a long paragraph on this point with these words:

How true is not this expression of Ambrose: "O the riches of Mary's virginity." [102] Of a truth, because of these riches it is of greatest value for today's virgins and religious men and women to contemplate Mary's virginity, that they may practice the chastity of their own state more faithfully and more perfectly. (*On Holy Virginity*, p. 188)

We should, therefore, study this mirror of spotless purity and often look into it, not merely in some impractical manner, but with a view to imitating it as closely as possible. St. Ambrose writes:

This is the image of virginity. For Mary was such that the example of her alone is a lesson for all. If, then, the author does not displease us, let us try the work, that whoever desires its reward for herself may imitate the pattern. How many kinds of virtues shine forth in the one Virgin! The secret of modesty, the banner of faith, the service of devotion; the virgin within the house, the companion for the ministry, the mother at the temple. (*On Virgins*, Bk. 2, Ch. 2, n. 15) [103]

Secondly, Mary the Virgin of virgins is the Mediatrix of perfect purity. From her we obtain the grace of vocation, from her we obtain all the graces needed to preserve that vocation. Our devotion to her should, then, include many a heartfelt "Thank you" for the gift of that vocation and for all other graces received for and because of it. But here we wish to lay emphasis on the importance of praying to her for the graces needed to protect purity. We should rely heavily on her all-powerful intercession with God's Son, her Son. When fleeing from occasions of sin, we should take refuge in the arms of our dearest Mother. Surely, she cannot turn a deaf ear to a sincere: "Remember, O most gracious Virgin Mary, that never was it known that anyone who fled to your protection or implored your help, was left unaided." It would be an excellent idea to recite this Memorare each morning for the gift of perseverance in one's vocation.

There is a very special relation between the virgin bride of Christ and her Guardian Angel. Those who live in perfect chastity, and especially virginal, as we noted earlier, begin an angelic life on earth. It is fitting that they should be associated with and imitate their guardian angels in the practice of virtues. The Guardian Angels were destined by God as the ministers of our salvation (cf. Hebrews 1,14). They are in a special way the custodians of virginal purity. It is profitable for virgin souls to call upon their Guardian Angels for help in preserving their purity undefiled. Their Guardian Angels will guide them in the way of prudence and guard them against dangerous occasions of sin.

The story of St. Cecilia contains a beautiful and inspiring lesson. She had made a vow of virginity, but she was also given in marriage to Valerian. The first night she addressed him in these words: "Valerian, I am under the protection of an angel, who guards my virginity. So, please, do nothing to me that will arouse God's anger against you." Valerian was so moved by her plea that he did not touch her, and even promised that he would believe in Christ if he could see that angel of hers. When Cecilia told him that was impossible unless he were baptized, he desired baptism, so anxious was he to see her angel. He was baptized by Pope Urban, and when he returned to Cecilia's house, he found her in prayer, and with her he saw her angel, all radiant. He told his brother, Tiburtius, about this, and he was baptized and was privileged to see Cecilia's angel.

We cannot, without a special privilege, see our angels with our bodily eyes; but we can know about their presence through faith. A strong faith in the reality and presence of our angels will give us confidence in their love for us and in their protection of our purity.

A very powerful means of preserving chastity and of perfecting it is to have a high ideal of this virtue. The old saying is: "Aim high if you wish to hit the mark." If you wish to remain chaste, you must set your ideals of chastity very high. This desire of ideal chastity is in itself a very long stride toward the possession of it. An ardent desire for a spiritual good is already a kind of possession of it and is a forceful means for gaining actual possession of it. One who is content at aiming at nothing higher than mediocrity in chastity will end by not being chaste at all. One who wishes to avoid only the bigger sins will sooner or later slide from smaller faults into bigger sins. To protect chastity untarnished one must have ideals.

For the greatest success, moreover, in observing chastity it is necessary to set one's ideals high not only in regard to chastity, but in regard to all the other virtues, in regard to everything in the spiritual life. The truth of this is borne out by the sad experience of some who lived a long time with no catastrophe in purity. Then, all of a sudden, it seemed, they fell headlong into sin. Was it so sudden? Not at all! The preparation for that was gradual, by carelessness in regard to the spiritual life in general, especially in regard to a spirit of prayer and of self-denial.

Of particular importance in striving to achieve our ideals is that we pay attention to small matters in the spiritual life. If we look only to practicing so-called big acts of virtue, and are careless about small things, especially about things that will escape the notice of others, we are running the risk of being unfaithful in chastity. The reason is simple: Purity is very much a matter of hidden virtue, and impurity, of hidden vice. One who has not acquired a sense of responsibility before God to be faithful in little things that are hidden from the eyes of men, will easily disregard practices of chastity that are hidden from fellow men. Test yourself: do you run risks of immodesty and impurity that you would not want to be known to your friends who have a high esteem of your virtue?

For protecting and perfecting purity it is of greatest value to keep on hand the strongest motives. The highest motive is, of course, the supreme excellence of consecrated chastity, based chiefly on the fact that the consecrated virgin is Christ's bride in a very special sense and degree. Always, then, keep in mind a vivid picture of the great dignity to which perfect chastity has elevated you. If you never lose sight of your consecration to Christ through chastity, it will be for you not so much the difficult commandment as the ever-beautiful, lily-like virtue that draws you on to greater heights of holiness.

Another motive is the Pauline idea that a Christian is a temple of the Holy Spirit:

Or do you not know that your members are the temple of the Holy Spirit, who is in you, whom you have from God, and you are not your own? For you have been bought at a great price. (1 Corinthians 6,19)

If that beautiful and inspiring mystic metaphor is true of every Christian, how much more so is it true of the virgin consecrated to Christ! The virgin must, then, guard against desecrating that temple. If Christians are to keep themselves chaste, as Paul explains earlier, because of their intimate union with Christ in the Mystical Body (1

Corinthians 6:15-16), how much more should not those remain pure who are consecrated members of that Mystical Body?

Not only the positive motives, however, have power for resisting temptations; the negative do, too. There arise situations in which the negative motives alone are strong enough to deter one from a serious violation. So it is worthwhile to recall in a general way the abominable evil that impurity is especially in one consecrated to Christ. Impurity is a specific degradation of the human person, body and soul, that is not had in any other sin, according to the inspired teaching of St. Paul: "Flee immorality. Every sin that a man commits is outside the body, but the immoral man sins against his own body" (1 Corinthians 6,18). True, impurity is not the greatest kind of sin theologically, but it has the most disastrous effects even for the theological virtues. It makes one frivolous, inconstant, not interested in heavenly things. It makes one ashamed of God and men. After Adam and Eve lost sanctifying grace, they lost also the sense of innocence, were ashamed of themselves, and hid from God. The unchaste person feels like hiding from God. The result is that he is inclined to conceal the sins in Confession. Impurity makes one spiritually blind. Impurity clamors for repetition more strongly than any other sin does. Even only half-hearted consent to impurity causes more worry and remorse than any other sin does. Live a chaste life, then, because of the abomination you would bring on yourself through impurity.

If it comes to the worst, the worst is eternal hell for an immoral life and a desecrated temple of the Holy Spirit. Let us never forget that divinely revealed truth. But let us be more mindful of the other divinely revealed truth that the reward for a sincere effort to live a chaste life is heaven and a clearer vision of the all-pure God's infinitely interesting and Holy Face. We spoke earlier of this heavenly reward in detail. How consoling is Christ's word to John: "Be faithful unto death, and I will give you the crown of life" (Apocalypse 2,10).

There is a spark of the "romantic" in every human heart. The faculty of loving someone is God-given and is essential to a human heart. Dedicating oneself to Christ in chastity does not take away this essential inclination. Every human heart must love someone. If by consecrated chastity one denies himself the intimate love of a fellow being in marriage, one must sublimate for that and substitute the love of Christ. This, in fact, one promises to do in consecrated chastity. If one does not love Christ, one will love a creature in spite of the promise not to.

One who is dedicated to chastity can best control the desire for forbidden love by the greater and more sublime love of Christ. The love of pleasure can best be cured by the excelling power of Christ's love.

Center, therefore, your love on Christ. Be interested in Him, your Spouse. How often do we not see a marriage broken up because of the lack of interest shown by one spouse in the other. If a person dedicated to chastity does not take an interest in Christ, if he does not take time out to converse with Him each day in prayer, Christ will let such a one on his own. If he does not bother about conversing with Christ after Communion, when He is so near, how can one expect Christ to help one in temptation?

This matter of being interested in Christ brings out the supreme value of a spirit of prayer for preserving purity. Without a spirit of prayer it is impossible to remain pure. By that we mean one must be interested in speaking with Christ even at times when one is not obliged to.

Interest in Christ means not merely that we love Christ, but that we love all else in and through and for Christ. The ceremony for the Consecration of Virgins says: "They love nothing outside of You [Christ]."

The Church Fathers insisted much on this truth, as we have had occasion to note. St. Ambrose never lets the virgin forget that she is consecrated to Christ. His *Exhortation on Virginity* is remarkable for the number of times that Christ is the center of his thought.[104] Elsewhere he insists that the virgin should "fully know Him whom she loves, and should acknowledge every mystery of" Christ.[105] He exhorts, too:

Love Him, my daughter, for He is good. For "no one is good but God only" (Luke 18,19). For if there is no doubt that the Son is God, and that God is good, there is certainly no doubt that God the Son is good. Love Him, I say. . . . (*On Virgins*, Bk. 3, Ch. 1, n. 3)[106]

St. Jerome, that great counsellor of virginity, tells the virgin Eustochius:

All that we have said will seem difficult to one who does not love Christ. But one who considers all worldly pomp as dung, and deems all things under the sun as empty, in order to gain Christ, and one who has died together with his Lord, and risen together with Him and has crucified his flesh with its vices and passions, will readily exclaim: "Who shall separate us from the love of Christ?" (Romans 8:35). (*Letter to Eustochius*, n. 39)[107]

To the noble virgin Demetrias he writes:

Happy is that conscience and blessed that virginity in whose heart there dwells no other love beside the love for Christ, who is wisdom, chastity, patience, and justice, and the other virtues. (*Letter to Demetrias*, n. 19) [108]

St. Augustine, after telling the virgins that they ought to love Christ as much as, or even more than, they would have loved a husband had they married—the passage was quoted earlier—adds:

It is not lawful for you to love only a little Him, because of whom you have not loved even what would have been lawful. So I have no fear of pride in you who love Him who is meek and humble of heart. (*On Holy Virginity*, n. 56) [109]

The Bishop of Hippo insists that the virgins follow Christ at present through imitation of all His virtues, especially purity, so that in heaven they may follow Him wherever He goes, according to the promise of the Apocalypse (14,4) (*On Holy Virginity*, n.27). [110]

Just as the Eucharist is the center of the Christian life and the primary source of perfection, so it is also the center of virginal purity and love. The topic is too vast to be treated in detail here. I should like to indicate only a few salient ideas.

As sacrifice the Holy Eucharist is the foremost source for acquiring a true sacrificial spirit for living in complete continence and generous love for Christ. It is the primary source from which to draw a genuine spirit of self-denial, which we showed to be so necessary for living chastely. It is the most sublime act in which the virgin can unite herself with Christ the Spouse and make the sacrificial offering of herself in total surrender to God through the vow of perfect chastity or virginity.

As sacrament the Eucharist can be considered a specific measure against impurity as well as a general means of fostering a more intimate life of love for Christ. That is what the Holy Father meant when he wrote:

> The more pure and chaste a soul is, the more it hungers for this Bread, from which it draws strength to resist every kind of allurement to impure sins, and by which it is more intimately united with the Divine Spouse: "He who eats my flesh and drinks my blood, abides in me and I in him" (John 6,57). (*On Holy Virginity*, p. 187)

As a specific measure against impurity Holy Communion is powerful for subduing the passions and diminishing concupiscence. It does that directly, as the great Suárez[111] and others teach, by moderating the lust of the flesh, refraining the imagination, and subduing the passions of the sentient appetite. That is why Leo XIII could say that the Eucharist is the best remedy against lust, an idea that Pius XII repeats (*On Holy Virginity*, p. 187).[112]

Holy Communion subdues the passions also indirectly by increasing grace, and especially the fervor of charity toward Christ; in other words, by fostering the positive side of consecrated virginity. The words put on the lips of St. Agnes are very appropriate: "His Body is united with mine; His Blood adorns my lips: His love renders me chaste; His touch purifies me; His coming secures my virginity." By increasing the fervor of charity the Eucharist perfects the union with Christ and deepens love toward Him. In that way it helps immensely to sublimate nuptial love and gives the soul a positive love to take the place of the human love that was renounced through perfect chastity. Moreover, for a few transcendent moments after Communion, the Bridegroom is present, not only by His grace, but personally, in the palatial temple of His bride, to share with her the most intimate love-union. How can Communion not be the divinely instituted instrument for perfecting consecrated chastity and love?

CHAPTER FIFTEEN

Social Life and Friendships

"TELL ME WITH WHOM YOU ASSOCIATE, AND I WILL TELL you what you are." This old adage expresses a profound truth. Our associates have a telling effect on our character. That is quite true of people who wish to live a single life in the world. Single life in perfect chastity creates a special problem in regard to companions and friends.

We spoke about some phases of the social life of such single people when we wrote of their apostolic work, careers, and homes. We noted several times that on no condition may bachelors and virgins live a common life for economic reasons. That must be an absolute rule. History painfully records the scandals and personal disasters that occurred in the early centuries of the Church because of disregard for this rule.

The single people will necessarily have contacts with others in their careers and apostolic work. They should be able to associate normally with others in society, without any abnormal emotional reactions, as for instance, undue bashfulness or fear or boldness. They should be calm and natural in conversation even with the other sex, and should guard against a fear complex in dealing with the other sex,

171

as if temptations lurked everywhere. In these contacts, which are for business purposes, they should be business-like always. They should not attempt to make an impression on the other sex, especially not by particular efforts to please them by their appearance. They should, it is true, be affable and neat and modest in appearance, but the primary intention for this should be to be pleasing to their Divine Spouse. Nor should they, on the other hand, be bold in putting themselves into occasions of temptations.

For the rest, the single will want contacts with others for the sake of friendship and recreation. Here they are at a disadvantage. The friends of their youth married and formed a new set of friendships with other married people. The single thus become somewhat isolated socially, and especially the women are soon classed with the "old maids." They should, however, not neglect a social life over and above their contacts through career and apostolate. True, Christ is to be their closest friend, but they are still entitled to some human friendships, provided they do not allow these to deteriorate into so-called particular friendships, namely, such as center interest on sensual and even sexual pleasures. Christ Himself had His special friends, the Apostles, and among these He had a still more special friend, St. John. Single people are allowed to cherish special friendships. It is natural that the first to have a claim on such friendships are near relatives. Since there is here scarcely anything peculiar to the single spouses of Christ, we need say no more.

It will certainly be advisable, too, to have friendships with some of the same sex who are following the same vocation, and who perhaps belong to the same parish society. Such friendships will offer mutual encouragement and spiritual consolation as well as legitimate relaxation. Further, bachelors and virgins for Christ's sake may well have other friends among those of their own sex, whether married or unmarried. Whether they should have friendships with non-relatives of the other sex, apart from business or professional purposes, calls for a lengthier discussion. Let it be understood that the following remarks are meant only for such single people who have definitively closed the door to marriage and have resolved to live a single life in perfect chastity. The remarks do not concern those who are single but who have not given up hope of marriage, and do not intend to.

Is it possible for two of opposite sex, when at least one of them has resolved to lead a life of perfect chastity, to foster a friendship that will remain platonic, that will not seek special sex attraction and desire sex satisfaction? To answer that adequately we must consider the nature of friendship and its consequent joy.

Friendship is not a chance, short-lived acquaintance or companionship. Friendship is mutual love that is based on a common possession of goods or characteristics and common interests, and that wishes well to the friend and will do well by him, especially if he is in need. It is, in other words, mutual benevolence and beneficence. Benevolence supposes a sympathetic understanding between friends; beneficence calls for a spirit of sacrifice for the good of the friends. Such friendship expresses itself in these acts: a friend wills that his friend retain the good he already possesses and takes great delight in his friend's possessing that good, praises it, congratulates him on it; he desires that the friend receive all other good that he does not possess but can possess; he sorrows over the loss of any good that the friend sustained; he lends a helping hand to the friend whenever opportunity and especially need presents itself; he desires to be ever more closely united with the friend. It stands to reason that one is not a friend if he helps his "friend" to sin. To do well by a friend means to help him to be morally good and achieve his greatest happiness, and not to do him the grave spiritual harm of pushing or pulling him into sin.

Friendship is essentially in the intellectual faculties of the soul. The intellect cognizes the friend and his attributes, and the will loves them and takes delight in them. All this is possible even in the natural order, namely, without grace. But it is perfected in the supernatural order. When sanctifying grace adorns the soul, and actual grace supports the mind, and supernatural reasons motivate the will, then we have supernatural friendship. Such friendship exists, for instance, between young Catholics of the same sex. To stress the fact that friendship can exist only in the intellectual faculties and to distinguish it from sentient love, we can style it spiritual friendship.

Since man is made of body and soul, and since he has not merely intellectual faculties but also sentient faculties whereby he can cognize the physical qualities of a person and love them, man can love another with a sentient love. Sentient love is more demonstrative than spiritual love. It tends to manifest itself in external signs of affection. Such sentient love is followed by sentient delight. Both sentient love and delight are unmixed, pure, when not influenced by, or influencing, spiritual love and joy, or sexual love and pleasure. For instance, one can love and delight in the fragrance of a rose or in the sound of Beethoven's Fifth Symphony, or in the touch of velvet. Such unmixed sentient love and delight is in itself morally indifferent, neither good nor bad. It becomes either good or bad according as the will uses it for a good or a bad purpose. When used for an evil purpose it is termed sensual pleasure.

Because man is a composite of body and soul, spiritual love can easily be mixed with sentient love. The step from pure spiritual love to sentient love is short and easy. Spiritual love redounds to sentient love; but sentient love can strengthen and intensify spiritual love. A mother's spiritual love and joy in meeting her daughter after a long absence redounds to sentient love and delight that expresses itself in a tender kiss and a warm embrace, and is itself strengthened by these.

There is in the sentient appetite a special appetite for using the power of sex to the fullest in the legitimate act of conjugal love and for enjoying its pleasure. Such use and enjoyment of sexual pleasure is lawful only between two who are lawfully married to each other. There is a close connection between sentient love and delight and sexual love and pleasure. Theoretically and practically they are quite distinct and may never be confused as far as moral values are concerned. And still they are closely related, because both reside in the same sentient faculty, and sexual love and pleasure can be stimulated even strongly by acts of the sentient faculties that are pleasurable, as seeing, hearing, touching, and that have by their nature at least an indirect stimulating effect on sexual pleasure. Those sentient pleasures that have scarcely even remote stimulating force on sex in normal people, but are indulged in for their own sake, not for the sake of sexual pleasure, are called sensual. These pleasures, though not sexual in themselves, and though not intended as a means to sexual pleasure, can easily lead to sexual pleasure.

Besides the localized pleasure from the sense of touch anywhere in the body, there can be a more or less general sentient delight of feeling in the whole body. This arises from the stronger motion and pressure of the blood, because of the increase of the heart beat and breathing and various reactions of the nerves and muscles. Such a delight may be caused, for instance, by one's expecting a person, or by sharply focusing a person on the imagination, and still more by the actual presence of a person that gives sentient delight, or spiritual delight that overflows into the sentient faculty. This common sentient delight, mixed with spiritual delight or unmixed, must be judged morally by the principles laid down for any sentient delight. It, too, can be related, even closely, to sexual pleasure. Again, the same principles hold then as for any sentient pleasure that influences the sexual appetite or pleasure indirectly.

When the mutual love of friendship and the sentient love and delight to which it redounds are between two of opposite sex, there can be and almost always will be present, at least in a slight degree, a love of the distinctive, at least secondary, characteristics of the other sex. As is known the two sexes have different physical, mental and moral characteristics that complement each other. So if one loves someone of the other sex, his or her love will almost necessarily center somewhat on the qualities that are complementary to his or her own. Though this is neither theoretically nor practically special sexual love, it has a quality different from that between two of the same sex, precisely because it is based on the special personality traits that are due to the difference of sex and that complement one's own traits. This love could be called *general* sexual love or attraction.

Such general sexual love can be either spiritual or sentient or both, and the consequent delight can be spiritual or sentient or both. When one's love centers on qualities that are cognized by the senses and desired by them, namely, the physical features and qualities, then the love is sentient, and the delight consequent upon that love is sentient. For instance, a man will love in a woman her beauty, her gracefulness, her "sweet" voice. A woman will love in a man his protective strength and masculine voice. Sentient love likes to express itself externally, by kissing, embracing, and caressing. The sentient passions can and do assert themselves rather strongly, we assume here, in a good sense. Such unmixed sentient love is morally an indifferent matter, in itself neither good nor bad. It becomes either only inasmuch as the will uses it for a good or a bad end. When the will uses it to strengthen and intensify spiritual love and joy which is morally good, then sentient love and delight are good. If the will uses it to make more vehement the spiritual love and joy which are morally bad, then the sentient love is bad.

This general sexual love is spiritual when the interest is in mental or moral qualities, namely, in the qualities that are cognized by the intellect and loved by and enjoyed in the will. It is of the head and heart, inasmuch as these are symbols, respectively, of intellectual knowledge and love. The resultant joy will be truly spiritual satisfaction in the possession of its object. The will calmly enjoys the intellectual and moral, natural and supernatural, qualities of the other. When this love is unmixed with sentient love, there are no sentient or bodily demonstrations of affection. A man, for example, loves in a woman her mental intuition, her tenderness, her maternal sympathy, her generous devotion, her emotional receptivity. A woman loves in a man his calm deliberation, his creative mental energy, his courage, his paternal protective spirit. Such love is emotionally calm and reserved, though not emotionless. It enjoys the presence of the other but is not restless when absent. When this love is mutual and has all the other characteristics of true friendship, as outlined above, it is genuine, even supernatural, friendship.

It does not take very profound thinking to make one realize that, though sentient love and friendship, as just described, between two of opposite sex, are not to be confused with sexual love and pleasure in the special sense, there is a very close relation between the two, precisely because the love and joy is based on the differentiating traits of the sexes, and also because there is a close connection between the sentient love and the sexual appetite, which resides in the sentient appetite, and is readily stimulated by sentient actions.

That outline of friendship and love should help one to see what is possible and what allowed in the line of friendship and love toward one of the other sex by one who is dedicated to a single life of perfect chastity.

Let us look at the matter from the view point of the purpose of such love or friendship. There may be no friendship for the sake of dating with a view to cherishing a love that might lead to marriage. That would be directly against the promise of perfect perpetual chastity. So there may be no expressions of affection, kisses, caresses, embracing, such as are usual and legitimate between lovers. Such behavior would soon sound the death knell to interest in virginal life. Nor is there any place for flirtation by one who has determined to have only Christ as Spouse.

Again, friendship should not be sought in order to overcome the peculiar loneliness that results from the lack of a marriage partner. A certain amount of loneliness is necessarily connected with the vocation of the single life in chastity. Christ alone, who was chosen as Spouse, can fill the void of such loneliness in the human heart. If one were to seek friendship with one of the other sex to overcome that loneliness, in all probability the friendship would be very dangerous to purity, or at least it would end in marriage.

But should the single seek such friendships as a means of complementing each other's character traits? There is certainly no need for that. One's personality can be essentially quite complete without the friendship of one of the other sex. Such a friendship, on the other hand, could have some accidental benefits for character development. But that leads to the crucial question. Is such friendship possible, namely, in the spiritual field and supernatural order, which might redound to the sentient love and delight and be strengthened by these, without deteriorating into special sexual love? Some are quick to answer that such friendship is possible and practical. One might note what Canon Sheehan has to say in his excellent *Triumph of Failure:*[113]

It has been said often, let me repeat it for the 100th time, that the best grace a young man can receive in life is the friendship of a good woman. And there is no clearer indication of the depths of vulgarity and degradation into which we have fallen than the universal idea that there can be no such friendship that does not degenerate sooner or later into sensuous affection. The universal presumption that marriage is the be-all and end-all of woman's life tends to ennervate natures that are of themselves strong and self-reliant. . . . It is impossible to calculate the heart suffering and martyrdom of women who believe they can have but one vocation in life, and whose views of men are restricted to that one idea.

All must admit, I believe, that Canon Sheehan has succeeded admirably in showing that such friendship is possible in fiction. His creation of the personality of Miss Helen Bellamy, who had no inclination to marriage, and whose friendships even with men were of the genuine intellectual and spiritual kind, is "ideal." Her friendship would be inspiring to anyone.

And still for real life one could make too general a statement about the possibility or advisability of such friendships, just as one might be too general in denouncing their possibility. A golden mean would seem to be correct.

Perhaps, granted that such friendships are possible, the problem must be solved with each friendship that might arise. A person may be able to foster a friendship on the platonic plane with one, but not with another. And surely there are some emotional types that could scarcely keep a friendship with anyone of the other sex on a high plane, though they can live a chaste single life if they avoid such friendships.

One must admit, further, that, regardless of how perfect the friends are, or how lofty the motives of friendship, there are at least remote dangers in them, and one must be prudent enough to take the proper precautions and not to allow the remote dangers to become proximate, and to break off the friendship if the danger should become proximate.

It is a matter of fact that we are not living in paradise with the gift of immunity from ill-regulated passions. Though spiritual love and sentient love, held within bounds, are quite legitimate, emotion cannot be excluded from such love; and from emotion to passion is often a very short step, and slippery, because of our fallen nature with its ill-regulated passions. We have grace, thanks be to God, but grace does not free us from temptations. It helps us to overcome them. It supposes that we make the effort to avoid occasions of sin. We do not wish to say, however, that the presence of some temptations in a friendship is a sign that the friendship should be broken off immediately. There are temptations in every walk of life. And yet, when such a friendship should be a proximate occasion of losing one's vocation to the single life of perfect chastity, it must be given up. It is that, when it becomes an absorbing interest, so that one is always thinking of the friend when absent, and is restless for the friend's presence, and longs to hear the friend's voice and to see the friend's face. Then it is certainly high time to break off the friendship, because it will become more absorbing, without being able to be satisfied, short of giving up one's vocation of single chastity.

It is well to know that even though a friendship begins on a high plane of spiritual interests, it can deteriorate to sensual and even sexual interests. And the more a friendship is based on purely recreational interests, the more liable is it to deteriorate to sexual love.

Women must realize that they are physically and sexually passive in relation to man, who is active. That means that a man's sexual appetite is more easily and strongly aroused than a woman's, with the result that what may be as yet no real danger to a woman may be a proximate danger to a man. A woman may, therefore, insist that a certain friendship with a man is very platonic, but that may be only from her side. To the man it could be a proximate occasion for sexual love, and indirectly also a danger to her.

One who dedicates his life to Christ in perpetual chastity is expected to, and does, strive for greater perfection in all virtues, and should because of that be a better person in every respect. He has a more winning personality. But just that can be a very attractive bait for a friend who might still be looking for a marriage partner. A friendship with such a one would be a danger to the vocation of single chastity. It should be clear that the dangers we are speaking of are not all immediate risks to purity. They may be simply occasions for one to drift away from the ideal of a single life of chastity and end by getting a dispensation from a vow, if one was made, in order to get married.

If the friend happens to be a married person, the dangers multiply. There is then danger not merely to the two friends, but there is a liability that the partner of the married friend will be injured, or will have occasions for jealousy. And this danger is so much greater when the marriage is not proceeding too happily. So, if there would be a friendship between a single person and a married person, it should always include the partner of the married person. There may never be any so-called dates with the married person alone. It would never do for a person to promise to give up marriage for life to live in perfect chastity and then to be instrumental in breaking up the happiness of a home, because one is not generous enough to be detached from dangerous friendships. It should, of course, not even have to be mentioned that such a friendship can never be tolerated with a divorced person.

It is necessary, too, to avoid scandal in this matter. If it is known publicly that one has chosen the single life of perfect chastity, people would soon be scandalized if they would see the single person too often with "dates."

Granted, then, that a determined friendship with one of the other sex is possible, and realizing that there is always a remote danger that such a friendship may deteriorate into sensual and even sexual love if not controlled, one must be constantly on guard and train oneself well in the science of resisting the very beginnings of any temptations, especially by building up a genuine spirit of self-denial and detachment from temporal pleasures, for the sake of loving Christ more wholeheartedly. One should learn to seek consolation and friendship chiefly in Christ and His all-pure Virgin Mother. The bride of Christ may never forget that she is espoused to Christ, and has surrendered her love to Him alone.

By way of appendix to this problem of friendships for the single I should like to say a few words about their recreations. Even though the single spend many hours on a career and in the active apostolate, and have a regular program of prayer, there will usually be some time left, and there should be, for relaxing the muscles and nerves. One can spend that time of recreation alone or with friends.

Depending on what type of work one does for a career or for the apostolate, there is a varied field in which one may find legitimate recreation according to one's tastes and talents. One may wish to ply a hobby at home. A man may enjoy cabinet making. A woman may find great delight in sewing or knitting. Materials so made or re-made could be used for helping the poor. Some may like to cultivate a little garden or to raise house flowers, which are both very refreshing hobbies. Again, one may take an interest in books, either by way of wholesome recreational reading, or for solid study. A little of this each day in a particular field will, over the years, yield a store of information. Adult education programs, extensive as they are today, offer excellent opportunities for spending after-office hours profitably. Then there is the possibility of doing some writing for publication, either in newspapers or magazines, or in books. The fine arts, of course, always offer special occasions for leisurely and recreational occupation. One may have a knack for painting, another for playing a musical instrument. Others may like a good drama. Finally, some may take to sports for their recreation, either by watching them or by taking an active part in them, or by coaching others. Whatever it may be, let it be a help to serving and loving Christ more ardently and energetically, and let it be for His glory and honor.

Prayer to My Divine Spouse

O Christ Jesus, Divine Spouse of mine, I express my most heartfelt gratitude to You for having chosen me, unworthy as I am, for the great privilege of "following You wherever You go," and of sharing in Your richest graces on earth and most intimate glory in heaven.

That I may be more worthy of Your great goodness, I now dedicate myself anew to live in perfect chastity to the end of my life out of love for You. I beg of You to help me to preserve untarnished, and to perfect still more, the lily of purity. Through Your favor, I will strive earnestly to avoid all sins of immodesty and impurity. Aided by Your Spirit of Holiness I will improve myself constantly in the technique of resisting temptations and in the skill of avoiding occasions of sin. I beg of You, my Spouse, the unmerited favor of a love for You that will daily become more intimate and more wholehearted, so that my converse with You already on earth may be a pleasant paradise. Though trials of all kinds might engulf me, help me to persevere in loving You patiently, cheerfully, hopefully—You who have loved me to the point of dying for me.

May I work out my salvation diligently in every virtue and every duty as long as it is Your good will for me to remain in exile from You. At the same time, may I desire the day of my death as no earthly spouse has ever longed for the wedding day. Indeed, that will be my final wedding celebration of glorious beauty and heavenly joy. May my departure from this world be the entrance to the never-ending vision of Your loveliness, and to the union of love and communion of joy with You, the Immortal King of the Ages.

Good Jesus, Lover of my poor self, grant me the courage so to live that I may be worthy of the great dignity You have bestowed on me of being Your very spouse. Most especially, may I receive You frequently in Holy Communion to strengthen and purify my love for You. And please, dear Jesus, may my converse with You in Holy Communion be a foretaste of that blissful life with You in heaven. Amen.

FOOTNOTE REFERENCES

Chapter One

1. *Discorsi e panegirici* (1931-1938), (Milan, Vita e Pensiero, 1939), 633-634.

Chapter Two

2. Denzinger, *Enchiridion Symbolorum* (Freiburg in Br., Herder, 1953), n. 980.

Chapter Three

3. *Acta Apostolicae Sedis*, 37(1945), 287.
4. *Ibid.*, 35(1943), 134.
5. *Ibid.*, 46(1954), 163. Hereafter, when quoting from or referring to the Encyclical *On Holy Virginity*, only the title will be given, with the pagination from this volume of the *Acta*.

Chapter Four

6. Cf. St. Cyprian, *On the Apparel of Virgins*, n. 20 (Migne, *Patrol. latina*, 4, 459).
7. St. Athanasius, *Apologia ad Constantium*, Ch. 33 (Migne, *Patrol. graeca*, 25, 640).
8. St. Ambrose, *On Virgins*, Bk. 1, Ch. 8, n. 52 (Migne, *Patrol. latina*, 16, 202).
9. Cf. *Ibid.*, Bk. 3, Ch. 1-3, nn. 1-14 (Migne, *Patrol. latina*, 16, 219-224); *Idem, On the Instruction of a Virgin*, Ch. 17, nn. 102-114 (Migne, *Patrol. latina*, 16, 333-336).

10. Cf. St. Cyprian, *On the Apparel of Virgins*, Ch. 4 and 22 (Migne, *Patrol. latina*, 4, 443-444 and 462); St. Ambrose, *On Virgins*, Bk. 1, Ch. 7, n. 37 (Migne, *Patrol. latina*, 16, 199).

11. St. Augustine, *On Holy Virginity*, nn. 54-55 (Migne, *Patrol. latina*, 40, 428).

12. St. Methodius, *The Banquet of the Ten Virgins*, Discourse 11, Ch. 2 (Migne, *Patrol. graeca*, 18, 209).

13. St. Augustine, *On Holy Virginity*, n. 27 (Migne, *Patrol. latina*, 40, 411).

14. St. Bonaventure, *On Evangelical Perfection*, q. 3, a. 3 (Quaracchi edition, Vol. 5, 176).

15. St. Fulgentius, *Letter 3*, Ch. 4, n. 6 (Migne, *Patrol. latina*, 65, 326).

16. *The Life of the Virgin St. Euphrasia*, Ch. 2 (*Acta Sanctorum* of the Bollandists, 1865, tome 2, 263).

17. Pope St. Siricius, *Letter 10*, to the Bishops of Gaul (Migne, *Patrol. latina*, 13, 1182).

18. Migne, *Patrol. latina*, 2, 911.

Chapter Five

19. Cf. *Acta Apostolicae Sedis*, 19(1927), 138.

20. St. Thomas, *Summa Theologica*, Part 2-2, q. 152, a. 3, o. 4; St. Bonaventure, *On Evangelical Perfection*, q. 3, a. 3, s. 5 (Quaracchi edition, Vol. 5, 178).

Chapter Six

21. Migne, *Patrol. latina*, 16, 198.

22. *Acta Apostolicae Sedis*, 42(1950), 791.

23. St. Augustine, *On Holy Virginity*, n. 9 (Migne, *Patrol. latina*, 40, 400-401).

24. For *Menti nostrae* see *Acta Apostolicae Sedis*, 42(1950), 663.

Chapter Seven

24a. *On Catholic Working Women of Italy*, Discourse of August 15, 1945 (*Acta Apostolicae Sedis*, 37[1945], 214).

25. Discourse of October 21, 1945, *On Women in Social and Political Life* (*Acta Apostolicae Sedis,* 37[1945], especially pp. 288-293).

Chapter Eight

26. St. Bonaventure, *On Evangelical Perfection,* q. 3, a. 3 (Quaracchi edition, Vol. 5, 176).

27. Cf. *Acta Apostolicae Sedis,* 42(1950), 610; Didymus of Alexandria, *Against the Manicheans,* 9 (Migne, *Patrol. graeca,* 39, 1095).

28. St. Bonaventure, *On Evangelical Perfection,* q. 3, a. 3 (Quaracchi edition, Vol. 5, p. 175).

29. St. Ambrose, *On Virgins,* Bk. 1, Ch. 11, n. 65 (Migne, *Patrol. latina,* 16, 206).

30. *Ibid.,* Bk. 2, Ch. 2, n. 18 (Migne, *Patrol. latina,* 16, 211).

31. Cf. *The Banquet of the Ten Virgins,* Discourse 5, Ch. 1, 4, 6, and 8 (Migne, *Patrol. graeca,* 18, 97, 101-104, 108, 112).

32. *Ibid.,* Ch. 1 (Migne, *Patrol. graeca,* 18, 97).

33. *Ibid.,* Discourse 7, Ch. 3 (Migne, *Patrol. graeca,* 18, 128-129).

34. St. Gregory the Great, *Homilies on the Gospel,* Bk. 1, Homily 3, n. 4 (Migne, *Patrol. latina,* 76, 1089).

35. Pius XI, in *Enchiridion Clericorum* (Herder, 1938, n. 1458).

36. St. Cyprian, *On the Apparel of Virgins,* Ch. 22 (Migne, *Patrol. latina,* 4, 462).

37. Tertullian, *To His Wife,* Bk. 1, Ch. 1 and 4 (Migne, *Patrol. latina,* 1, 1276 and 1281).

38. He is quoting St. John Damascene, *On Orthodox Faith,* Bk. 4, Ch. 21 (Migne, *Patrol. graeca,* 94, 1210).

39. Cf. *Acta Apostolicae Sedis,* 42(1950), 580.

40. St. Augustine, Migne, *Patrol. latina,* 40, 410.

41. St. Ambrose, Migne, *Patrol. latina,* 16, 199.

42. *Loc. cit.*

43. *Summa Theologica,* Part 2-2, q. 152, a. 5.

44. St. Augustine, Migne, *Patrol. latina,* 40, 428.

45. Cf. *Mary Mediatrix, Encyclical Letter, Ad diem illum* of Pope St. Pius X, translated and annotated by Dominic J. Unger, Capuchin (Paterson, N.J., St. Anthony Guild Press, 1948), p. 16 f.

Chapter Nine

46. St. Augustine, Migne, *Patrol. latina*, 40, 439.
47. *Idem, ibid.*, 407.
48. *Ibid.*, 407.
49. *Ibid.*, 438.
50. *Ibid.*, 446.
51. *Ibid.*, 445.

Chapter Ten

52. St. Methodius, Migne, *Patrol. graeca*, 18, 44, 45.
53. St. Athanasius, *On Virginity*, cf. the edition of Th. Lefort, in *Muséon*, 42(1929), 247.
54. St. Augustine, *Sermon 51*, Ch. 16, n. 26 (Migne, *Patrol. latina*, 38, 348).
55. See, for instance, Joseph Mueller, S.J., *The Fatherhood of St. Joseph*, translated by Athanasius Dengler, O.S.B. (St. Louis, Herder, 1952), p. 64 f.
56. St. Athanasius, *On Virginity*, edition as in Note 53, p. 244.
57. St. Ambrose, *On the Instruction of a Virgin*, Ch. 14, n. 87 (Migne, *Patrol. latina*, 16, 328).
58. *Idem, On Virgins*, Bk. 2, Ch. 2, nn. 6 and 15 (Migne, *Patrol. latina*, 16, 208 and 210).
59. *Ibid.*, Ch. 3, n. 19 (Migne, *Patrol. latina*, 16, 211).
60. *Idem, On the Instruction of a Virgin*, Ch. 7, n. 50 (Migne, *Patrol. latina*, 16, 319).
61. *Ibid.*, Ch. 13, n. 81 (Migne, *Patrol. latina*, 16, 339).
62. Cf. *Mary Mediatrix, op. cit.* (in Note 45), p. 7.
63. Cf. Sister M. Thérèse, Ed., *I Sing of a Maiden: The Mary Book of Verse*. New York: Macmillan Co., 1947, p. 336.

Chapter Eleven

63a. *Acta Apostolicae Sedis,* 35(1943), p. 247.

64. Clement of Jerusalem, Migne, *Patrol. graeca,* 8, 300-301.

65. St. Methodius, *The Banquet of the Ten Virgins,* Discourse 11, Ch. 2 (Migne, *Patrol. graeca,* 18, 212).

66. *Ibid.,* 72-73.

67. *Ibid.,* 73.

68. St. Ambrose, Migne, *Patrol. latina,* 16, 197.

69. St. Augustine, Migne, *Patrol. latina,* 40, 399.

70. St. Cyprian, *On the Apparel of Virgins,* Ch. 3 (Migne, *Patrol. latina,* 4, 443).

71. St. Methodius, Migne, *Patrol. graeca,* 18, 72-73.

72. St. Augustine, Migne, *Patrol. latina,* 35, 1459.

73. *Idem,* Migne, *Patrol. latina,* 33, 848 f.

74. *Idem,* Migne, *Patrol. latina,* 40, 400-401.

75. St. Ambrose, Migne, *Patrol. latina,* 16, 197.

76. Origen, Migne, *Patrol. graeca,* 12, 181.

Chapter Twelve

77. St. Ignatius, Migne, *Patrol. graeca,* 5, 717.

78. *Ibid.,* 724.

79. *Ibid.,* 653.

80. St. Polycarp, Migne, *Patrol. graeca,* 7, 1009.

81. St. Justin, Migne, *Patrol. graeca,* 6, 349.

82. Athenagoras, Migne, *Patrol. graeca,* 6, 965.

83. St. Theophilus, *To Autolycus,* Bk. 3, n. 15 (Migne, *Patrol. graeca,* 6, 1141).

84. See Note 81.

85. See Note 82.

86. See *On the Ornament of Women,* Bk. 2, Ch. 9 (Migne, *Patrol. latina,* 1, 1326); *To My Wife,* Bk. 1, Ch. 6 (*ibid.,* 1283); *On the Veiling of Virgins,* Ch. 10 (*ibid.,* 2, 903); *On the Exhortation to Chastity,* Ch. 13 (*ibid.,* 2, 930). See Vizmanos, *op. cit.,* p. 127.

87. St. Augustine, *On the True Religion*, Ch. 3, n. 5 (Migne, *Patrol. latina*, 34, 125).

88. Cf. *First Letter*, Introd. (Funk, *Patres Apostolici*, Vol. 2, p. 2); Ch. 3, n. 1; Ch. 7, n. 2 (Funk, 2, pp. 2 and 6).

89. The testimony is found in Kirch-Ueding, *Enchiridion fontium historiae ecclesiasticae antiquae*, 5th edition, Freiburg, 1941, n. 154.

90. Cf. Note 19.

Chapter Thirteen

91. Published by Queen's Work, St. Louis, 105 pp.

Chapter Fourteen

92. St. Methodius, Migne, *Patrol. graeca*, 18, 220.

93. *Pratica di amar Gesù Cristo*, Ch. 17, nn. 7-16.

94. The Pope quotes St. Jerome, *Commentary on Matthew*, 19, 11 (Migne, *Patrol. latina*, 26, 135), and St. Ambrose, *On Virgins*, Bk. 3, Ch. 4, nn. 18-20 (Migne, *Patrol. latina*, 16, 225).

95. Cf. St. Caesar of Arles, *Sermon 41* (edition of G. Morin Maredsous, 1937), Vol. 1, p. 172.

96. St. Thomas, *Commentary on 1 Corinthians*, Ch. 6, Lecture 3; St. Francis de Sales, *Introduction to a Devout Life*, Part 4, Ch. 7; St. Alphonsus Liguori, *The True Spouse of Christ*, Ch. 1, n. 16; Ch. 15, n. 10.

97. St. Jerome, *Against Vigilantius*, 16 (Migne, *Patrol. latina*, 23, 352).

98. St. Augustine, *On Holy Virginity*, Ch. 54 (Migne, *Patrol. latina*, 40, 428).

99. St. Methodius, *The Banquet of the Ten Virgins*, Discourse 6, Ch. 3 (Migne, *Patrol. graeca*, 18, 117).

100. St. Ambrose, *On Virgins*, Bk. 2, Ch. 2, n. 14 (Migne, *Patrol. latina*, 16, 210).

101. *Idem, On the Instruction of a Virgin*, Ch. 6, n. 46 (Migne, *Patrol. latina*, 16, 320).

102. *Ibid.*, Ch. 13, n. 81 (Migne, *Patrol. latina*, 16, 339).

103. *Idem, On Virgins*, Bk. 2, Ch. 2, n. 15 (Migne, *Patrol. latina*, 16, 210).

104. *Idem*, Migne, *Patrol. latina*, 16, 266-302.

105. *Idem, On Virgins*, Bk. 1, Ch. 9, n. 46 (Migne, *Patrol. latina*, 16, 201).

106. *Ibid.*, Migne, *Patrol. latina*, 16, 221.

107. St. Jerome, Migne, *Patrol. latina*, 23, 423.

108. *Idem*, Migne, *Patrol. latina*, 22, 1123.

109. St. Augustine, Migne, *Patrol. latina*, 40, 428.

110. *Ibid.*, 411.

111. Suárez, *Commentary on Part 3 of the Summa theologica*, q. 79, d. 64, s. 1, n. 5; De Lugo, *De Eucharistia*, d. 12, s. 4, n. 87.

112. Leo XIII, Encyclical *Mirae caritatis*, May 28, 1902 (*Acta Leonis XIII*, Vol. 22, pp. 1902-1903; and *Acta Sanctae Sedis*, 34(1901-1902, 646).

Chapter Fifteen

113. Canon Sheehan, edition of Burns and Oates, London, 3rd edition, p. 43.

If you have enjoyed this book, consider making your next selection from among the following . . .

Prices subject to change.

Visits to the Blessed Sacrament. *St. Alphonsus*. 5.00
Moments Divine—Before the Blessed Sacrament. *Reuter* 10.00
Miraculous Images of Our Lady. *Cruz*. 21.50
Miraculous Images of Our Lord. *Cruz*. 16.50
Saints Who Raised the Dead. *Fr. Hebert* 18.50
Love and Service of God, Infinite Love. *Mother Louise Margaret* 15.00
Life and Work of Mother Louise Margaret. *Fr. O'Connell* 15.00
Autobiography of St. Margaret Mary. 7.50
Thoughts and Sayings of St. Margaret Mary. 6.00
The Voice of the Saints. *Comp. by Francis Johnston* 8.00
The 12 Steps to Holiness and Salvation. *St. Alphonsus*. 9.00
The Rosary and the Crisis of Faith. *Cirrincione & Nelson* 2.00
Sin and Its Consequences. *Cardinal Manning* 9.00
St. Francis of Paola. *Simi & Segreti*. 9.00
Dialogue of St. Catherine of Siena. *Transl. Algar Thorold* 12.50
Catholic Answer to Jehovah's Witnesses. *D'Angelo* 13.50
Twelve Promises of the Sacred Heart. (100 cards) 5.00
Life of St. Aloysius Gonzaga. *Fr. Meschler* 13.00
The Love of Mary. *D. Roberto*. 9.00
Begone Satan. *Fr. Vogl*. 4.00
The Prophets and Our Times. *Fr. R. G. Culleton* 15.00
St. Therese, The Little Flower. *John Beevers* 7.50
St. Joseph of Copertino. *Fr. Angelo Pastrovicchi* 8.00
Mary, The Second Eve. *Cardinal Newman*. 4.00
Devotion to Infant Jesus of Prague. *Booklet*. 1.50
Reign of Christ the King in Public & Private Life. *Davies* 2.00
The Wonder of Guadalupe. *Francis Johnston*. 9.00
Apologetics. *Msgr. Paul Glenn* 12.50
Baltimore Catechism No. 1 . . . . 5.00
Baltimore Catechism No. 2 . . . . 7.00
Baltimore Catechism No. 3 . . . . 11.00
An Explanation of the Baltimore Catechism. *Fr. Kinkead* 18.00
Bethlehem. *Fr. Faber*. 20.00
Bible History. *Schuster* 16.50
Blessed Eucharist. *Fr. Mueller*. 10.00
Catholic Catechism. *Fr. Faerber* 9.00
The Devil. *Fr. Delaporte* 8.50
Dogmatic Theology for the Laity. *Fr. Premm* 21.50
Evidence of Satan in the Modern World. *Cristiani*. 14.00
Fifteen Promises of Mary. (100 cards) 5.00
Life of Anne Catherine Emmerich. 2 vols. *Schmoeger.* (Reg. 48.00) 40.00
Life of the Blessed Virgin Mary. *Emmerich*. 18.00
Manual of Practical Devotion to St. Joseph. *Patrignani* 17.50
Prayer to St. Michael. (100 leaflets) 5.00
Prayerbook of Favorite Litanies. *Fr. Hebert* 12.50
Preparation for Death. (Abridged). *St. Alphonsus*. 12.00
Purgatory. (From *All for Jesus*). *Fr. Faber* 6.00
Bible History. *Johnson, Hannan, Dominica*. 24.00
Fundamentals of Catholic Dogma. *Ludwig Ott* 27.50
Spiritual Conferences. *Faber*. 18.00
Trustful Surrender to Divine Providence. *Bl. Claude* 7.00
Wife, Mother and Mystic. *Bessieres* 10.00
The Agony of Jesus. *Padre Pio* 3.00

Prices subject to change.

At your Bookdealer or direct from the Publisher.

Toll-Free 1-800-437-5876   ***Fax 815-226-7770***
Tel. 815-226-7777   ***www.tanbooks.com***

Prices subject to change.

Fr. Dominic J. Unger, O.F.M. Cap. 1907-1982

Father Dominic J. Unger, O.F.M. Cap. was born in 1907 at Herndon, Kansas. After a year of novitiate, he entered the Capuchin Order in 1928 at Herman, Pennsylvania. He was ordained to the priesthood in 1934. After completion of his priestly studies in 1935 at Washington, D.C., he was sent to Rome for higher studies. There he received the licentiate in theology from the Gregorian University in 1936 and the licentiate in Sacred Scripture in 1938. Upon completion of another year of studies as a candidate for the doctorate in Scripture from the Pontifical Biblical Institute, he returned to the United States, where he taught theology and Sacred Scripture until 1950. Subsequently, Fr. Unger spent many years in research and writing, facilitated by his knowledge of Franciscan history and Mariology, as well as his knowledge of 14 languages—modern, classical and middle-eastern. He also did much pastoral work, including serving as a "weekend assistant" in various parishes.

Besides numerous articles for Catholic periodicals, both scholarly and popular, Fr. Dominic Unger wrote several pamphlets and a number of books, including *Handbook for Forty Hours Adoration, The First Gospel: Genesis 3:15, Our Lady's Daily Hours,* plus offprints from the *Collectanea Franciscana*, including *The Absolute Primacy of Christ Jesus and His Virgin Mother according to St. Lawrence of Brindisi,* and *The Heavenly Queenship of God's Virgin Mother according to St. Lawrence of Brindisi.* Fr. Dominic Unger translated *Against the Heresies* by St. Irenaeus of Lyons, and he was actually one of the three translators of what is known as the Kleist-Lilly translation of the New Testament. Many of his other writings, on a wide range of topics, remain unpublished. In 1960 he was chosen by Pope

John XXIII to be a consultor to the Theological Commission preparing for the Second Vatican Council; he participated by correspondence. In his later years, Father wrote against the errors and excesses of false forms of "renewal."

Fr. Unger went to his eternal reward in 1982, after suffering patiently from stomach cancer for about a year. His funeral took place on the 50th Anniversary of his permanent profession as a Capuchin. A tribute published at that time includes the following reflections on Father Dominic Unger's life and personality:

"No matter what assignment he was given, he accepted it obediently and put himself into it fully." He was a many-sided man who loved classical music, played the violin, and was also a skilled butcher, carpenter, bookbinder, parliamentarian and inventor, as well as a good conversationalist and considerate adversary. He was at home with scholars but was happy to associate with all. Fr. Dominic is remembered as a holy and humble friar. His final resting place is in St. Joseph Cemetery in Hays, Kansas.

Grateful acknowledgement to Fr. Blaine Burkey, O.F.M. Cap. for much of the material in this life sketch.